The Instant Sales Director

The INSTANT Sales Director

Ready from Day One

John D. Moulton

CASTLE
HOUSE
Publications

First published 2026

ISBN: 979-8-9947421-0-5 (Paperback)
ISBN: 979-8-9947421-2-9 (e-Book)

Published by
Castle House Publishing

First Edition

CASTLE
HOUSE
Publications

Your Journey Ahead

PART ONE

SO MANY HIDDEN TRUTHS

The realities, disciplines and decisions that
determine who is ready to lead - and who isn't.

How great sales people break through to sales leadership

Preparing Your Pathway Ahead
Taking a hard look in the mirror, sharpening your CV and cover letter, and
positioning yourself for opportunity - before it appears.

Winning The Interview Game
Preparation, psychology, post-interview leverage, and why some interviews fail
- even when you do everything right.

Day One and Beyond - Leadership Realities
Your entry into the business. Meeting your sales force and customers.
Handling the most important sales meeting of your career. Working with the
sales office. Hiring and firing people.

Building the Engine - Leading Like a Professional
Marketing realities. Delegation. Time Management, Communication - and the
disciplines that separate managers from leaders and transforming culture
where others merely endure it.

PART TWO

LESSONS LEARNED THE HARD WAY

Stories from the field that reveal what
theory never teaches - and experience never forgets.

Truths earned in the trenches

Stories that put weight behind the words.
Some amusing. Some uncomfortable. All essential.
Here to provoke thought and challenge assumptions…
and remind you that experience is the most expensive education of all.

CONTENTS

Part One

Part Two

DEDICATIONS

To every manager I ever worked with.
You all helped shape the leader I became.

Thank you.

To Tom Peters, who's amazing works, particularly for me: *"In Search of Excellence", "A Passion For Excellence"* and *"The Circle of Innovation"* had me realise, firstly that I wasn't mad to think the way that I thought, and mostly for the guidance those books offered at the time I needed them most.

To the late, **Kenneth JD Quinn,** a man brave enough to allow me much leverage while seeking a new path for his company. For his courage in handing me control of product design, marketing and sales, and for being a true friend in a personal moment of great need. Rest in peace Ken, you were one in a million.

Introduction

Most people who aspire to senior sales leadership don't fail through lack of effort or ambition.

They fail because the route is poorly explained.

Sales management is often presented as something you either grow into or qualify for through credentials. In practice, neither guarantees readiness – and both can leave capable people stalled, overlooked, or unprepared when opportunity finally calls.

This book exists to close that gap.

It is written for people who already understand sales, who care about doing the job well, and who want to move into positions where they can influence outcomes rather than merely respond to them.

Some readers will be preparing for their first senior role. Others may already hold one and recognise, with hindsight, how little practical guidance they received along the way.

What follows is not theory-heavy training, and it is not a motivational manifesto. It is a practical guide built around real decisions, real pressures, and real consequences – the kind that arise in interviews, on the first day in the role, and in the weeks and months that follow.

You won't find jargon. You won't be asked to memorise frameworks that collapse under pressure. Instead, the book breaks the journey down into clear stages, highlighting what matters at each point, what commonly goes wrong, and how to avoid learning everything the hard way.

Read it straight through, or dip into the sections most relevant to where you are now. Either approach works. The material is designed to be absorbed gradually and applied immediately.

If your aim is to move into senior sales leadership with clarity, confidence and a grounded understanding of what the role actually demands, then this book is written for you.

Let's begin.

Getting Ready For The Road Ahead

The Starting Line - and exactly what 'Instant' means:
Before anything else, it's worth being clear about what instant means in this context.

This book will not: Propel you effortlessly into a boardroom overnight. **What it will do** is ensure that when opportunity appears, you are ready for it. Prepared for the questions, the expectations, and the realities of senior sales leadership – not just how to secure the role, but how to hold it once you do.

Preparation matters: Getting the job is one challenge. Keeping it, growing into it, and earning the confidence of those around you is another altogether.

The pages that follow are designed to give you that preparation. They focus on readiness rather than fantasy, clarity rather than bravado, and understanding rather than slogans. By the time you reach the end, the path ahead should feel familiar rather than intimidating. You'll be ready, day one, to walk into your new position, quietly confident. A calming presence, **instantly ready for the road ahead.**

This first section marks the starting line:
Here, we'll look honestly at where you are now, what will be expected of you, and how to prepare yourself for the road ahead.

Some of the questions asked may be uncomfortable. That's deliberate. They are the kind of questions senior roles demand long before anyone asks them out loud.

These early section heads offer a brief synopsis of the tasks and the mindset that sales directorship demands.

All will be examined in much greater detail as we progress.

Are You Ready For Leadership?

You probably wouldn't be reading this if you weren't preparing for, or discovering what the role really demands. The better question is: do you already have the raw materials for the role – and if not, are you willing to develop them quickly?

Do You Have What it Takes?:
A common mistake is to assume that the highest achiever on the sales team automatically makes the best sales director. Sometimes they do. Often they don't - because the disciplines are different.

The best coaches are not always the best players:
It's an old truism in sports as well as business. Before you set your sights on the role, ask and answer the questions below honestly. Not for me - for yourself.

- Are you a people person – with compassion and respect for others?
- Can you lead a team and work as part of one, with strong communication skills?
- Do you present yourself well – appropriately for your trade and your market?
- Are you organised?
- Are you a competent administrator (or willing to become one)?
- Can you listen, absorb, and shape the thinking of others for the benefit of the business?
- Do you care about quality and service – not just short-term numbers?
- Are you willing to go the extra mile when it matters?

Notice what I haven't asked! Whether you're a brilliant presenter, or a natural deal-closer. For now, we can assume you have solid sales ability – because sales directorship is built on something much broader than personal sales performance.

If you can answer "yes" to most of the questions above, you're already on the right track. If some of your answers are uncomfortable, the question becomes simpler: are you willing to improve?

A quick word about marketing:
In many companies, the sales director also carries responsibility for marketing. If that may be true in your case, add a few more questions:

- Are you an ideas person?
- Do you have an eye for design and presentation?
- Do you think reasonably creatively and strategically?

Even if your company outsources design or advertising, you still need a feel for what will work – and the ability to recognise a good idea when it's put in front of you.

If you feel weak in any of these areas, don't be discouraged. The aim of this book is not to flatter you; it's to prepare you. Most of what matters here comes down to attitude, temperament, and disposition – and those can be developed.

Your next step:
Take five minutes to consider each question: Make notes of your strongest areas, and circle your weakest. No one else will see this – but it will give you a clear starting point.

In the next section, we'll begin turning those raw attributes into practical, day-to-day behaviours you can carry into interviews and into the role itself.

Getting it on Record

The Paperwork – and why it matters:
Sales administration and reporting are disciplines most salespeople dislike. They want to be out selling. Paperwork feels like friction – a distraction from the real work.

Surely the orders speak for themselves?
Surely a quiet day doesn't mean a wasted one?

Those reactions are understandable – but they're also limiting.

Here's the reality: for anyone aspiring to sales directorship, this is a discipline you must embrace.

The good news is that many competitors for the role you're seeking feel exactly the same way you do. The bad news is that avoiding administration will doubtless remove you from contention. Used properly, reporting doesn't hold you back – it distinguishes you.

Your customer record:
If right now you deal with customers directly, you need a personal customer information record – regardless of what systems your company already uses.

This isn't a questionnaire, and it isn't intrusive. It's a working document built gradually and conversationally.

Make it a habit – It pays in spades.

Include:

- preferred name
- key personal details (partner, children, interests)
- buying patterns
- outlet profile   (Cont'd)

- staff relationships
- what worked last time
- what to address next time

After each call, note:

- what you achieved
- what you learned
- what you intend to do next

Over time, this becomes far more than admin. It becomes leverage.

Something you can do now:
If you already complete reports of any kind, take time to review them. Ask yourself what you would add, remove, or reshape to make them genuinely useful. You don't get to abandon reporting altogether – that's not an option – but you do get to improve it.

If you currently have no structured reporting, sketch what should exist for your role: performance indicators, qualitative notes, and short-term targets that go beyond raw numbers.

No one else needs to see this. The value lies in the thinking.

One critical thought:
If the idea of structured reporting and record-keeping genuinely repels you – or if you simply refuse to engage with it – then you should give serious thought to whether sales directorship is the right ambition for you.

This discipline isn't optional at the top, it's mandatory.

I expand on this subject under the heading, *'Meaningful Reporting'* in Part Two.

Team Leader, Team Player

The phrase team leader, team player isn't new – and for good reason. It sits at the heart of effective sales management. What varies wildly in the real world is how seriously it's understood, how consistently it's applied, and how well the balance is managed.

So let's be precise about what it actually means.

Rule One – Selling is a people business:
Sales has always been a people business. That applies just as much to leading a sales team as it does to dealing with customers.

You won't get far in sales unless people are willing to engage with you. That doesn't mean they have to like you all the time – we've all bought from people we didn't particularly warm to – but in those cases we usually wanted or needed, the product badly enough to overlook the relationship.

That's not Salesmanship …

That's order-taking.

As a sales director, your first task is to sell yourself - not just to a board of directors, and not just to customers, but to your team. If they don't buy into you, they won't fully buy into your direction.

This book isn't about teaching you how to sell. But some elements of selling are inseparable from leadership, because influence always precedes authority.

Rule Two – Leadership requires participation:
People approach leadership from many angles.

At one extreme are the authoritarian managers who insist on compliance – my way or the highway. At the other are those who confuse being liked with being effective, hoping goodwill (being nice) alone will produce results.

Neither approach works for long.

People tolerate oppressive management for many reasons: fear of change, financial dependency, lacking the confidence to move on. But very few give their best under it – and those who do usually succeed despite their manager, not because of them.

At the opposite extreme, over-accommodation leads to blurred standards, inconsistent performance, and inevitable disappointment – often for the very people the manager is trying to protect.

The answer lies between the two.

One reality you must accept:
You are not good enough to do this job on your own.

If you are already in a management role and rely on command, compliance, or fear to get results, you should stop and reassess. Respect cannot be demanded – it can only be earned.

Equally, if you routinely defer difficult decisions, excuse underperformance, or allow standards to slide in the name of harmony, you should be clear about where responsibility ultimately lands when results suffer.

Leadership is neither domination nor indulgence. It is responsibility.

Where authority really sits:
The most effective team leaders are able to engage closely with their people. They listen. They invite challenge. They allow space for disagreement – including opinions that are uncomfortable or critical.

But they are also clear about one thing.

Once people have been genuinely heard, once they know their views have been considered, the final decision must rest with you. And the team must understand – and respect – that responsibility.

That clarity is not oppressive. It is reassuring.

A moment of reflection:
Consider how you currently lead – or how you intend to.

- Where do you sit between authority and accommodation?
- Where do you listen well?
- And where do you avoid decisions?

You don't need to answer these questions out loud. But you do need to answer them honestly.

We'll return to management style in much greater depth later. For now, recognise this: effective leadership is not about control, and it's not about popularity. It's about trust, clarity, and accountability – starting with your own.

I expand on this subject under the headings, *'Putting Your Sales Force on a Pedestal'* and *'Getting Close to the Team'* in Part Two.

Quality Service – Theirs and Yours

This should be one of the shortest sections in the book. In an ideal world, it wouldn't need to exist at all.

Unfortunately, it does.

The emphasis here is deliberate. This is not about quality and service as abstract ideas, or about criticising companies for the products they make. It's about *quality service* – and your role in delivering it.

You, are part of your company's offer:
How you present yourself, how you behave, and how you engage with customers all shape how your company is perceived.

Your appearance, demeanour, sales materials, and even the condition of your car form part of the shop window customers see every day. None of this is new – but it is remarkable how often it's neglected.

Leading an on-the-road sales force:
As a sales director, your responsibility extends beyond your own conduct. Everything above applies equally to the people you lead.

In theory, this should be straightforward. People tend to mirror what they see. If you set a clear standard and live it consistently, most will follow.

That said, leading others is not the same as performing well yourself. There is an assumption throughout this book that you already know how to sell. What comes next is about ensuring others can do so effectively – and consistently – under your direction.

The success of your sales force is your success. Unless you're a one-person team, the two cannot be separated.

Responsibility for the Sales Office

If your experience so far has been primarily field-based, the sales office arena may feel unfamiliar, even a little uncomfortable, but it's importance should not be underestimated.

A sales office has its own disciplines, pressures, procedures and hierarchies. Whether staff are actively selling or simply taking orders, their performance has a direct impact on customer experience and sales outcomes.

In most offices there will be a supervisor or manager. That individual can quickly become either an ally or an obstacle.

We'll return to this in more depth later. For now, recognise that responsibility for the sales office, in one form or another, may fall within your remit – and its performance will affect yours.

A Practical Reflection

Take a moment to consider your own standards.

- Are you presenting yourself as well as you could?
- Does your environment reflect the professionalism you expect?
- Are opportunities being missed through indifference or habit?

Pay attention not only to your own behaviour, but to how others sell and serve in general around you every day. Retail environments, exhibitions, offices, and your personal dealings as a customer. Make notes. Observe what works, what doesn't, and why.

If you intend to be a great sales director, this kind of observation shouldn't feel like work. It should feel like preparation.

Ability & Opportunity

Ability matters – but it's only effective when it's applied in the right environment.

This is one of the lessons it took me decades to understand completely. You now have the opportunity to benefit from that knowledge far more quickly.

Choosing your platform:
Early in my own career, I allowed companies to choose me. Any company would do. I believed loyalty meant staying put, nose to the grindstone. Moving on was something people simply didn't do.

That thinking was inherited. For my father's generation, and those before him. They 'sold their soul to the company.' A long CV was a liability. Changing companies was seen as instability rather than ambition.

Then came a wake-up call.

Over dinner one evening with my secretary and her husband – a man in his mid-twenties – I congratulated him on securing a marketing manager role with a local authority. It looked, to me, like a job for life and told him so.

His response stopped me cold.

He had told them at interview that he was giving them three years.

At twenty, he had already decided which company he wanted to end up with, and what executive role he wanted to hold there by the age of thirty. He contacted that company directly and asked what qualifications and experience would be required. Then he set about acquiring them – qualification by qualification – role by role.

It didn't matter whether that specific job was available when he arrived. His career path would qualify him for several similar roles.

He hadn't chosen a single platform. He had chosen several.

Your skills:
It's time to look in the mirror, at how you work, and where you genuinely want to work. Make a private list of your own standards and expectations. Be honest.

Consider:

- Your ability to work independently
- Your willingness to put in extra time when required, often without immediate reward
- Whether your life partner genuinely understands the demands a senior role may bring
- Whether you see yourself as someone who leads pragmatically, develops others, and follows things through

I'm not asking about core sales ability. That is assumed. What matters here is 'fit'.

Your passion:
Now consider the product or service itself. Which industries genuinely interest you? Which products or services do you believe in? Travel, engineering, technology, health, fitness – whatever it is, write it down.

You will perform better, and last longer, promoting something you care about. The aim is to find yourself thinking: I can't believe they're paying me to do this. It matters more than many people realise.

Know this with certainty: ***Ability is nothing without opportunity.***

So be very sure that opportunity will be yours.

Early Preparation

The importance of 'The Fit'

This brings us back to the idea of platform.

The business world often leans on the phrase survival of the fittest, misquoting Darwin in the process. What Darwin actually described was the survival of the fit – not strength, but suitability.

The fit between an organism and its environment. When that fit no longer exists, survival becomes difficult to impossible.

The same is true of careers.

If you and the company you work with are poorly matched – in values, expectations, or opportunity – ability alone will not save the relationship.

Selecting your company:
Once you understand your skills and interests, focus on companies that align with them.

Size and branding are seductive. It sounds impressive to name a household brand you work with. But external perception and internal reality often diverge. Companies can trade on reputation long after culture has shifted.

Look deeper:
How does the company treat its people?
Does it see sales as a strategic asset or a necessary inconvenience?
Is success celebrated – or merely demanded?

Some of this can be discovered from customers. More can be learned from people inside. At the very least, research what's publicly available: recent performance, stability, direction of travel.

Remember, too, that hiring often signals recognition that change is needed. You may be the person to drive that change.

The rest comes down to the interview – and preparation for that arena is where we'll turn next.

A moment of reflection:
List the industries, companies, and environments that genuinely fit your skills and temperament. Don't rush this. Choosing the right platform will do more for your long-term success than raw ability ever will.

I return to this idea with a real-world scenario in Part Two, under the heading, *Ability meets Opportunity,* where theory meets consequence.

Your CV/ Resumé

Your CV earns you the interview. It is your first filter – and you should treat it as such.

Before we get into format and structure, one point needs to be made clearly.

Skip the 'mission statement':
Many CV templates encourage a "Mission Statement" or "Objective Statement" at the top. In practice, these are often filled with recycled corporate phrases and fashionable buzzwords. Interviewers skim them at best – and will sometimes discard an application purely because it sends early signals of cookie-cutter thinking.

If you have something genuine to say about why you want this role at this company, put it where it belongs: in your covering letter, written in your own voice.

If you are forced to complete a form with a box labelled 'Objective' or similar, keep it plain, specific, and human. One or two lines. No slogans.

What your CV must do:
Your CV should be a fair, accurate summary of who you are and what you've achieved, presented in the most positive, honest light.

Two practical points:

- **Make achievements visible.** If your CV looks dull, you will be assumed to be dull, too.
- **Don't lie, and don't disguise gaps.** If your career includes short roles, handle them with simple honesty. If asked, explain what you learned without bitterness.

If you are unemployed at the moment, meaningful voluntary work can help – not as a 'patch', but as evidence of energy, character, and ongoing engagement.

About photos:
In some industries and countries, a photo on a CV is normal. In others, it is discouraged. Use judgement.

If a photo is appropriate in your market, make it a good one – a simple, professional portrait. People remember faces more easily than bullet points, and anything that helps an interviewer recall you positively can work in your favour.

A useful alternative to 'mission statements':
If you want a short opener at the top of your CV, replace the mission statement with something more practical:

A short heading such as *'My Career to Date – in Brief'* A few lines that summarise your experience, strengths, and the direction you're now aiming for, written plainly, in your voice.

That will do far more for you than any fashionable declaration ever will.

A moment of reflection:
Pull up your current CV and look at it as an interviewer would.

- Does it sound like a real person?
- Are achievements clear and specific?
- Anything there simply because a template told you to include it?

If you fix only one thing, fix this: ***make it sound like you!***

Your Covering Letter

... and Any Other First Approach:
Your CV may get you noticed – your covering letter gets you taken seriously.

Formats change. Platforms evolve. The underlying purpose does not. Whether you're writing a formal letter, an email, a LinkedIn message, or completing an online form, this is your first real conversation with a future employer – and it deserves care.

What this communication is really for:
The purpose of a covering letter (in any form) is not to repeat your CV – It is to **frame it.**

It should answer three unspoken questions in the reader's mind:

* Why this company?
* Why this role?
* Why you – now?

If you can do that clearly and concisely, you are already ahead of most applicants.

Making your case:
Everyone starts somewhere. The person reading your application has made a journey of their own, and very few began at the top.

If your background includes hard-earned experience rather than formal management credentials, that is not a weakness – provided you know how to present it.

Imagine this scenario:
Your application sits beside one from a business graduate applying for their first management role. Their CV lists education and poten-

tial. Yours lists experience, results, and time spent dealing with real customers and real consequences.

The difference is subtle – but you must make it visible.

You are not trying to diminish anyone else. You are simply making clear what you bring to the table: hands-on sales experience, people skills, judgement under pressure, and the ability to translate intention into action.

You haven't criticised anyone. You've simply reframed readiness.

Writing the letter – whatever the format:
The medium may vary, but the principles don't.

* Keep it to one page.
* State the role you're applying for clearly.
* Focus on the company's needs, not your frustrations.
* Be enthusiastic - but precise.
* Be honest about your background, and confident about your value.
* Translate experience into benefits for the business.
* Close positively, without begging.

Avoid opening every paragraph with "I". It subtly centres the wrong thing.

Above all, make sure it sounds like you. A letter that reads smoothly out loud will almost always read well on the page.

Proofreading matters more than you think:
Read your letter slowly. Then read it out loud. If you stumble, rewrite the sentence. If you need to take a breath, adjust the punctuation.

Then let someone else read it – not to flatter you, but to catch what you've missed. Spelling mistakes, awkward phrasing, and sloppy structure are among the easiest reasons for an application to be rejected.

Employers are often looking for reasons to narrow the field. Don't give them one.

Modern routes in:
Email, LinkedIn, online portals, and recruitment platforms are now routine. That doesn't mean they should be treated casually.

Short-form messaging, poor grammar, and conversational shortcuts have no place in a senior application.

If emailing, consider attaching a clean, well-formatted letter and CV rather than pasting everything into the body of the message. Test how it prints. What looks neat on screen can look careless on paper.

If contacting someone directly, make sure you know who you're writing to – and why. Generic approaches addressed to "whom it may concern" rarely lead anywhere useful.

Following up:
A few days after submitting an application, it's reasonable to follow up politely to confirm receipt. If you speak to someone directly, keep it brief and professional.

You are not chasing. You are signalling seriousness.

Your online presence:
Assume that employers will look you up. Some do it themselves. Others pay for it to be done.

What they find doesn't need to be flawless – but it does need to be sensible.

Professional platforms such as LinkedIn should reflect your working identity clearly. Personal social media accounts are best set to private while you're actively applying. If you choose to build a personal website, keep it simple, professional, and accurate.

The aim is not to impress everyone. It's to avoid undermining yourself.

A moment of reflection:
Before sending any application, ask yourself one question: *If I were reading this alongside twenty others, would it sound real?* If the answer is yes, you're ready to send it.

You and Your
Highly Qualified Competitors

An analogy worth keeping in mind: An engineer may know every component of an engine – every bolt, every tolerance. *But until they've learned to drive*, that knowledge remains theoretical. You, on the other hand, have learned to drive. You know how to keep the vehicle on the road, handle corners, and adjust to conditions as they change.

That is the distinction you are drawing – without arrogance.

A powerful positioning move:
If you are competing with candidates who already hold management titles, you can still create advantage without attacking them.

A simple line such as:

"I come ready to learn your company's ways and apply them without the burden of inherited habits."

Such words plant a quiet seed. It invites the reader to consider whether experience always arrives without baggage.

Before The Interview

You got the call. The interview is on.

Ideally, you have a few days to prepare. If you've already done the groundwork – researching the company and thinking carefully about the fit – you'll approach this meeting from a position of strength. If not, now is the time to catch up.

An interview is not just about whether the company wants you. It's about whether you want the company. The best interviews are two-sided conversations.

Getting there – properly prepared:
If the interview is local, do a trial run. Travel at the same time of day, on the same day of the week if possible. Check parking, access points, and the correct entrance. Large sites can easily catch people out.

If you can't visit in advance, call reception. Ask practical questions:

- parking availability and cost
- distance from parking to entrance
- the correct building and/or door

None of this is over-preparation. It's professionalism.

Don't rely blindly on digital journey estimates. They assume ideal conditions. Build in generous margin. It's far better to arrive early and wait than to arrive late and apologise.

Which brings us to something else important:

Final Preparation

- Two days before the interview (or sooner if possible):
- Gather all paperwork and complete any forms
- Print extra copies of your CV and covering letter
- Bring a notebook and pen – a slim clipboard folder looks organised without fuss
- If you keep personal sales records or logs, bring them if they're relevant and clear
- Everything you carry should reinforce one message: you are prepared.

The day before the interview:
Clean your car. Tidy the interior. Lay out your clothes. Fill the fuel tank.

These aren't vanity points. They remove friction and reduce last-minute stress. And occasionally, they're noticed.

You want nothing pulling attention away from the conversation that matters.

Final thoughts:
An interview is not an ordeal. It's a meeting.

If you prepare properly, arrive calmly, ask intelligent questions, and listen carefully, you give yourself the best possible chance – not just of being offered the role, but of deciding whether it's right for you.

The Interview

It's the morning of the interview:
If you're nervous, that's no bad thing. Many accomplished performers experience nerves before stepping on stage – and often say that those who don't feel nervous at all rarely give their best performances.

Your task today is simple:
To meet the challenge with composure and leave having represented yourself well.

Before you leave:
Give yourself time.

Dress appropriately for the company and the level of the role. Pay attention to the small things – shoes, hands, grooming. Make sure everything you need is ready and waiting by the door.

Nothing increases confidence like removing last-minute friction.

The Critical Five-Minute Rule:
Arrive five minutes early – not twenty or thirty. And not one minute late.

Five minutes early signals respect for the interviewer's time. It shows planning without pressure. Arriving too early can make people feel rushed; arriving late almost always leaves a mark.

Five minutes gives you room to settle, breathe, and deal with small surprises – like an unattended reception desk – without stress.

If something genuinely delays you, call ahead immediately. Keep the explanation factual and brief. When you arrive, acknowledge the delay once, apologise, and move on. Don't let it dominate the opening minutes of the interview.

Handling small stresses calmly is part of what's being assessed.

On the way:
Use the journey to visualise the opening moments. See yourself arriving calm and collected, confident without being forceful.

If the interviewer is not a sales professional, be especially mindful of balance. Confidence should feel reassuring, not overwhelming. Your aim is to convey capability – not urgency.

The Interview

First contact:
When you meet, offer a warm, professional greeting. A firm handshake, eye contact, and a clear introduction by full name.

If the interviewer offers their preferred form of address, remember it and use it naturally. These small signals matter.

This is not a contest for control, and it's not an exercise in deference. Think of it as **leading from the back foot** – allowing the interviewer to feel in charge, while subtly guiding the tone and substance of the conversation.

A useful early question is:

"Can you give me an idea how long we have to talk?"

It signals respect for time without suggesting you're eager to leave.

Understanding who you're dealing with:
Interviewers vary widely in experience and skill.

Some are structured, clear, and purposeful. They'll outline the role, explore your history, and test your thinking. These interviews feel focused and productive.

Others are less sure of what they're looking for. They may rely on impressions rather than analysis, or assume competence without probing for it. This isn't a criticism – it's a reality.

In interviews like these, it becomes your responsibility to ensure that important ground is covered. That doesn't mean taking over. It means guiding the conversation so that your capabilities – and the company's expectations – are clearly understood on both sides.

Taking responsibility for clarity:
There are two questions you must answer for yourself during every interview.

First:
What do you need the interviewer to understand about you?

Prepare this in advance. Know the key strengths, experiences, and perspectives you want to convey. If they don't surface naturally, introduce them gently:

"There are a couple of areas I think would be valuable for you to understand about how I work – may I talk you through them?"

That's professionalism, not pushiness.

Second:
What do you need to know about them?
This is just as important. Winning a role that turns out to be a poor fit is no victory at all. Sometimes the right outcome is clarity – even if it means walking away.

This is where your questions matter.

Is the Role all it Claims to Be?

That's *not* a question you ask, it's one you carefully probe for. Titles can be misleading. A 'Sales Director' role does not always come with board director-level authority.

That may be fine – provided expectations, responsibility, and influence are aligned.

What matters is not the title, but whether you'll have the authority required to deliver what you'll be held accountable for.

If those two don't match, frustration follows quickly.

A meeting of minds:
At this level, the interview should feel like a meeting of minds.

Respectful. Open. Direct.

Everything should be discussable, with the exception of detailed pay and privileges at this stage. Authority, expectations, scope, and culture are all fair grounds.

Let the interviewer see that you are evaluating 'fit' just as carefully as they are. That signals maturity – not arrogance.

Pay and privileges:
Avoid raising pay or perks in the first interview unless the interviewer does so. Even then, keep the discussion high-level.

There will be time for detail later. Raising it too early shifts the tone in the wrong direction.

Asking Tough Interview Questions

Some questions require judgement. Choose only a few.

- Why is the position vacant?
- How long have people typically stayed in the role?
- To whom would I report?
- What does success look like here?

Ask these calmly, and only when the interview feels balanced.

If the answers feel evasive, that tells you something useful.

Preparing your questions:
Good interviews include good questions – asked, with respect – for the right reasons.

Your questions should focus on fit: between your standards, skills, and expectations, and the platform the company offers.

Examples:

- *"Quality matters to me. How would you position your product or service relative to your main competitors?"*
- *"What does a typical week look like in this role?"*
- *"What would you want the person in this role to have achieved after the first six months?"*

That last question is particularly revealing. It exposes expectations – and potential mismatches – early.

Each question should be preceded by a short statement that signals your values. That way, the question feels thoughtful rather than confrontational.

Handling Difficult Questions

You'll also be asked questions designed to probe judgement, self-awareness, and resilience. You don't need rehearsed speeches – but you do need clarity.

Answer Questions Before They're Asked:
Weaving key points as answers to tough questions can be done naturally during the conversation. That signals confidence and self-knowledge – and keeps you in control of the moment.

Every job you've held taught you something. Even the least relevant role can be framed positively if you focus on what it developed in you.

In Part Two, I delve deeper into this in the Section headed: *More on Those Tough Interview Questions*

Closing & Departure

As the interview draws to a close, reaffirm your interest – warmly.

Express clarity about what the role requires and how you could contribute. Leave as you arrived: composed, professional, and positive.

If the fit feels right, let that show. If it doesn't, trust your judgement.

Either way, you've done your job.

I expand on this subject under the headings, *'Those Tough Interview Questions'* and *'A Meeting of Minds'* in Part Two.

After The Interview

As soon as you leave, whether by car or train, etc., take out your notebook.

While the conversation is still fresh, make a few honest notes. This isn't about self-criticism. It's about professional calibration.

What to Refine

Ask yourself:

- Were there moments that didn't land as well as you'd hoped?
- Did any answers feel unclear, rushed, or under-developed?
- Were there points you overstated – or undersold?
- Did you forget to mention anything important?
- Were you fully prepared for everything you were asked?
- Did you ask enough questions – or too many?
- Were there expectations raised that you couldn't comfortably commit to on the spot?

Be candid. No one else will see these notes.

If something genuinely fell short, ask a simple follow-up question: Is this a skill or understanding worth developing for the future?

If the answer is yes, you've just identified a growth opportunity.

What to Build on

Now look at the positives.

- What was well received?
- Where did the conversation flow naturally?   (cont'd)

- Did the chemistry feel warm and professional?
- Were there moments when the interviewer seemed genuinely engaged or impressed?

These are strengths. Make a note of them. They should shape how you approach future interviews.

Follow Through

A brief follow-up message matters.

Thank the interviewer for their time and courtesy. Reaffirm your understanding of the role and your interest in contributing. Keep it professional, concise, and prompt.

This isn't flattery. It's good manners – and good positioning.

When an Offer is Made

An offer during the first interview is rare, and sometimes worth a second look for that very reason.

More often, offers come at a second or third meeting. At that point, expect details of remuneration, benefits, and practicalities to be presented clearly – and in writing.

You should already know when you could reasonably start. If you don't, think it through before you attend.

One important question to ask:

Before you leave, ask about initiation.

Specifically:

- Is there a formal induction or onboarding process?
- What does the company expect in the first days and weeks?
- If the answer is vague – or even if it's well defined – this is your moment to show organisational maturity.

You might suggest:

- Meeting key executives and internal teams on day one
- A tour of operations, distribution, and finance
- Time in the field with a strong sales representative
- Early meetings with key customers
- A first meeting with the full sales team once context is established

This signals planning, leadership, and respect for process – before you've even started.

A final thought:
Not every good interview leads to an offer.

That doesn't mean it wasn't successful.

If you leave clearer, more confident, and better prepared than when you arrived, the interview has already done part of its job.

The next section will explore why strong interviews don't always covert – and what that really means.

But just before that …

Let's stop for a moment

Before we go any further, pause for a moment.

Imagine you're in the interview.

The conversation has been thoughtful.

The tone feels professional.

Then you're asked:

"What would your first ninety days look like?"

Write down what your response would be right now.

Be honest. Don't polish it. Don't overthink it.

Then tuck your answer away somewhere safe.

We'll come back to your thoughts later.

You Didn't Get the Job

Why not?:
Rejection is part of the process. It always has been.

There are three broad reasons interviews don't convert into offers:

- Things that could have been done differently
- Things that went well and should be built upon
- Factors that had nothing to do with your ability at all

Understanding the difference matters.

The road to future success:
Every interview is a learning experience – not as a platitude, but as a practical truth.

Each one gives you material: insights into your presentation, your judgement, your readiness, and the kinds of organisations that truly fit *you*. Treat interviewing as a craft, not a hurdle.

And remember – if you are pursuing management or director-level roles, you are learning skills you will later utilise yourself. Interviewing others is part of leadership. What you experience now will inform how you conduct those conversations in the future.

Honing your presentation:
There is little difference between a strong interview performance and a strong sales presentation.

Yet many sales professionals never properly examine their own pitch. They develop a script, repeat it often enough for it to work occasionally, and assume inconsistency lies elsewhere.

I've watched capable sales people miss opportunities repeatedly – not through lack of effort – but through lack of reflection. Missed benefits. Poor timing. Weak responses to objections. Accepting rejection too early and moving on.

Interviewing is no different.

No one can step in and rescue a faltering interview for you. That's why post-interview reflection matters. Ask yourself honestly:

- What worked? — What didn't? — What would I change?

That process – repeated – is how confidence becomes competence.

The Unspoken Reasons

When it wasn't about you at all:
Some rejections have nothing to do with your performance.

This isn't an excuse list. It's context.

Read this section **after** you've done the self-analysis above – not instead of it.

The role was effectively filled already:

Some organisations are required to interview externally even when an internal candidate would be preferred. You may never have been in contention.

They questioned *your* long-term fit:
They believed – rightly or wrongly – that you wouldn't stay, or that the role wouldn't suit you once inside. Fit matters, even when it's imperfectly judged.

You were perceived as too strong:
Occasionally, capability intimidates. This can happen when the interviewer feels threatened, consciously or otherwise. It's not admirable – but it is real.

Age perceptions:
Too young. Too old. These judgements still happen, even when unspoken. If you suspect this may be a factor, it can sometimes help to address it casually and directly in future interviews.

How I once fort against this and won, is shared in the Part Two segment, *'The Interview - When it Seems all is Lost.'*

Gender bias:
It exists – sometimes overtly, sometimes silently.

Other forms of classification:
Some organisations operate under internal or external diversity targets. These can affect outcomes in ways candidates never see or hear about.

You don't need to approve of this reality – but you do need to recognise it.

Your online presence:
If they searched for you and didn't like what they found, the decision may already have been made. This was covered earlier – and it matters more than many realise.

The final analysis:
Be honest - but not harsh - with yourself.

If your skills weren't quite there yet, work on them. If something in the role didn't feel right, trust that instinct. If you're unsure why you were rejected, it's reasonable to ask – respectfully – what would have strengthened your application.

Not every good interview leads to the right job. Sometimes the right outcome is clarity.

The right platform for you exists. Your task is to be ready when it appears – and to recognise it when it does.

I expand on this subject from personal experience in the Part Two Segments, 'When All Seems Lost' and 'The Hidden Reason You Didn't Get The Job'.

Day One as Sales Director

Setting the Stage

Day one – or one-thousand and one – this section applies:
It is about forming habits, setting tone, and establishing how you will lead. Read it carefully. What follows can save you months of frustration – or confirm very early that you've made the right decision.

A note to incumbents:
If you are already in the post, working within an established organisation that does not operate as described here, you will need to learn how to speak the organisation's language before attempting change.

That is a delicate skill, and we'll return to it later. For now, stay with the principles.

Down to business:
Be clear about one thing from the outset:

If a company is unwilling or unable to offer you the opportunity to grow the business meaningfully, think very carefully about staying. Culture, authority, and intent matter more than title.

That said, many organisations will welcome the approach that follows - particularly if you have chosen well and values align.

Day One - in essence:
No two organisations are the same, but the fundamentals of a good first day are remarkably consistent.

Best case:
You are welcomed, introduced properly, given context, and shown how the business works. There is structure, curiosity, and support.

Worst case:
You're shown your desk, introduced to a few nearby faces, and left to 'get on with it.'

If the latter happens, don't panic – but do pay attention. Ask yourself early:

- Do they know what they want from me?
- Do they understand the role they've hired me for?
- Do they have the capacity – and intent – to embrace change?

If the answers are unclear, evaluate quickly whether this is a place you can succeed.

Have your own plan:
Never arrive on Day One without a plan.

Ideally, you've already discussed an outline with your new boss. If not, take the initiative before you start. This is not presumption – it's leadership.

Your plan should cover:

- Who you need to meet
- In what order
- And why

This alone will set you apart.

Your First Days

First priority:
Time with your direct superior and, where appropriate, the executive team. Your aim is to listen, understand expectations, and confirm the shape of your first weeks – *not* to announce change.

Second priority:
Introduction to the internal teams you will work with or lead – sales office, marketing, customer service. Brief, respectful, human introductions. Promise one-to-one conversations later – and mean it.

Third priority:
Time in the field with a strong sales representative – to observe.

Fourth priority:
Time alone with key customers, as soon as possible.

Finally:
A meeting with the full sales force – ideally after you've seen the business from the inside and the outside.

If your boss suggests meeting the sales force immediately, handle this diplomatically. If it's already arranged, accept it. If not, explain why you want more context first.

Putting substance behind the plan:
If you're given extended time with senior leadership on Day One, take it – but listen more than you speak.

Reaffirm that you have a view of the first three months, but that you're reserving judgement until you understand:

- how the business operates
- where it's constrained
- how quickly it can move

State clearly that you will return with considered proposals within a few weeks.

If promised access or tours are repeatedly postponed without good reason, take note. Early avoidance often signals deeper resistance.

Who you need to meet – and why:
You need early contact with:

- Internal teams you will lead or have strong alliances with
- Production or service delivery
- Distribution or client services
- Finance

Finance matters because it shapes credit, risk, and customer experience – all of which affect sales outcomes.

In every department, observe:

- attitudes to quality and service
- openness to improvement
- respect for customers

If you hear *"we're too busy for that,"* take it seriously.

Taking stock:
You may have been hired to improve what you're seeing. That's fine – provided you have the authority and backing to do so.

Be very clear about that.

Companies that need change can be led by very stubborn people. You need to be sure that hiring you isn't just a cosmetic exercise.

Ask yourself:

- Is there openness to change?
- Will leadership support difficult decisions?
- Do people believe improvement is necessary?

These impressions, formed early, are often accurate.

Summary:
Your role as sales director carries responsibility and influence. Make sure the authority matches the expectation.

If it doesn't, recognise it early - and learn from it.

Next, we'll look at:

- your day in the field
- your first customer visits
- and your initial meeting with the sales force

These moments set the tone for everything that follows.

Meeting the Sales Force

By Stages:
You only get one chance to make a first impression. This is one of those moments – and it's worth doing properly.

Before you sit at the head of a table and address the sales force, you need to understand what life is actually like for them. Meeting the team before you've spent any time in the field almost guarantees that what you say will be heard as abstract or naïve.

Get out there first.

Why the order matters:
If you arrive as the new sales director and speak confidently about targets, structure, or improvement without having seen the reality of the job, you risk being dismissed internally as someone who doesn't yet understand their world.

Equally, you don't want to present yourself as a newly-arrived expert with instant solutions. You are new. They know it. Acknowledging that – while showing that you're willing to learn – earns far more respect than certainty ever will.

Your first day in the field:
Ideally, you've arranged a day with a capable sales executive. If the role involves travel, ride with them. They know the routes, the customers, and the rhythm of the day – and shared travel creates space for conversation.

Begin lightly if needed, but move quickly into listening mode.

Listening and learning:
People generally like to talk about themselves. Your job is to listen – not interrogate.

Over time, you'll want to understand what motivates each person: family circumstances, pressures, ambitions, stability, concerns. None of this needs to be gathered quickly, and none of it should feel intrusive.

This is not idle curiosity. It's leadership intelligence.

Keep your notes private. Use them to understand, not to manipulate.

Keeping perspective:
Be careful what you offer in return by way of personal disclosure. Everything you share should be positive, measured, and appropriate.

Avoid dwelling on past grievances, former employers, health issues, or personal financial strain. You're setting a tone – and information, once shared, travels.

This isn't about distrust. It's about professionalism.

Talking business – carefully:
Before each call, ask about the customer you're about to meet. This tells you a great deal about how the sales executive thinks about their accounts.

At the door, be clear: you're there to observe. You will be introduced as sales director, but you will not interrupt or take over the visit – and you must keep that promise, even if it's difficult.

Think of yourself as a documentary maker rather than a participant. Today is about observation.

What to watch for:
Sales training will come later. Right now, pay closer attention to how customers respond than to how the salesperson performs.

Customers often volunteer more insight than you expect – particularly when curious about you. If you're new to the industry, say so. Emphasise your commitment to quality, service, and attitude. Product knowledge can be learned. Character is harder to teach.

A common and surprising occurrence:
Don't be surprised if a customer doesn't place an order while you're present.

Many buyers are uncomfortable doing so in front of a salesperson's manager. They don't want the impression that the salesperson has it easy – or that management may take the credit.

Often, the order comes later, privately. This is more common than many managers realise.

Keeping your ears open:
Listen carefully to comments made in passing:

- jokes
- complaints
- small digs
- throwaway remarks

Some should be addressed immediately. Others later. Some back at the office.

But none should be ignored.

As the day progresses, use these moments as conversation starters with the sales executive. You'll often learn far more once a buyer has opened the door.

Taking stock:
This day is reconnaissance – nothing more.

Observe the gap between:

- how the company sees itself
- how the sales force experiences it
- how customers talk about it

You may not like everything you see and hear. Make notes. Keep your own counsel.

One final exercise:
At the end of the day, that sales executive will no doubt speak with colleagues.

What do you want them to say about you? Not as flattery – as intent. Words worth aiming for:

- listens
- open-minded
- sincere
- fair
- focused on quality and service
- calm
- professional

Descriptions worth avoiding:

- know-it-all
- pushy
- detached
- dismissive
- took over
- lectured

Write your own list. Revisit it often.

Self-awareness is not vanity – *It's leadership.*

A Day with Key Customers

Now to your day out on your own.

Within your first week, you should aim to meet between two and four key customers – before that first formal meeting with your sales force. If this proves genuinely impossible, arrange those meetings one-to-one as soon as you can afterwards, but do not postpone them without good reason.

These conversations matter.

A different kind of meeting:
Make it clear to everyone involved – including yourself – that this is not a sales call. It's reconnaissance. A meeting of minds.

You're there to introduce yourself, to listen, and to understand how the company is really serving this customer – and where it could do better. Breakfast, brunch, or lunch works well. The tone should be relaxed, purposeful, and honest.

You are not there to defend the company.
You are there to understand it.

What you're really there to learn:
You are not there to discover what's working. You're there to uncover what isn't – and what could be improved.

You need to know:

- why your company is not their number-one supplier (if it isn't)
- what threatens that position (if it is)
- what would make things easier, smoother, more valuable?

Listen carefully as customers talk about:

- the product or service itself
- the sales representative
- delivery and reliability
- customer service
- accounts and credit control
- even the driver who turns up at the door

Every one of these elements affects your ability to sell.

Filtering what you hear:
Use judgment. Some customers will ask for the impossible – top quality, lowest price, flawless service, instant response.

But buried in even the most unrealistic wish list are truths worth understanding.

Price must reflect quality and service. If your company is leaning too heavily on reputation, history, or uniqueness to justify margins, competitors will eventually find a way in – often with slightly lower prices and noticeably better service.

This is where perspective matters.

A word on value and desire:
One of my own long-held beliefs is this:

Want trumps need – and both trump price where desire rules supreme.

Desire changes the rules of value.

In the UK, for example, a standard piece of Perspex measuring 18" × 4" × 3/16" costs very little. Yet personalised vehicle registration plates - often made from precisely that material - regularly sell for tens of thousands of pounds.

Why? Because ownership satisfies desire, not need.

The lesson for you is simple:
where products are perceived as interchangeable, price dominates;
where desire is created, value expands.

Where price really matters:
Of course, there's a flip side.

In true commodity markets - fuel, basic foodstuffs, undifferentiated services, price sensitivity is unavoidable. Here, only quality and service create separation.

"Yes, we may be 10% more expensive - but look what you get."

That argument only works when it's true.

Which leads to another principle worth remembering:

Excellence can only be achieved by exceeding the expected.

And remember – *expectations move. Constantly.*

And, as my long-time favourite business thinker, Tom Peters puts it:

"If you're not getting better faster than the other guy is getting better, then you're getting worse."

Your role in all of this:
Knowledge is power.

As sales director – the company's front-line interpreter – your job is to gather this knowledge, translate it into language the organisation understands, and help drive meaningful change toward better serving customers.

You are not there to criticise for effect.
You are there to clarify reality.

Much more on how to do that – particularly how to speak their language – later in the book.

For now, absorb everything your customers share with you.

Because next, you'll be sitting down with your sales force for the first time – and what you've learned here will shape everything you say.

Your First Sales Meeting

The Opening Statement:
"Good morning, everyone.
For those I haven't met yet, I'm John - and John is fine."

(Pause. Eye contact.)

"Before I say anything else, I want you to know this:
I didn't want to meet you until I'd been out there."

"I've spent time in the field.
I've spoken with customers.
I've listened – far more than I've talked."

"What that's shown me is this:
You're doing a tough job in a tough environment – and there's good
work happening here."

(Pause - let that land.)

"My role is simple to state and hard to do well:
to make your job easier, not harder.
To remove obstacles.
To help you win more often – with less friction."

"I'm good at what I do – but I'm not good enough to do this alone.
I need your experience, your honesty, and your insight if we're going
to move this business forward properly."

"So here's how I work – briefly."

(Key shift: brief)

"I start from trust.
I value straight talk.

I listen carefully.
And when a decision has to be made, I'll own it."

"You'll always know where you stand with me – and I expect the same in return."

(Pause.)

"That's enough from me for now."

"Let's go round the table.
Tell me who you are, how long you've been here, and the patch you cover."

"Then we'll take a short break – and when we come back, we'll talk about what's ahead."

Now sit down. (Other matters arising)

Break for refreshments.

After the break:
When expectations become standards.

If your opening was about trust, this session is about clarity.
If the first meeting answered "Who are you?", this one answers "How will we work together?"

This is not the moment to get tougher.
It is the moment you get precise – there is a world of difference.

Setting the tone:
This is not a pep talk.
It is not a disciplinary meeting.
And it is not the place for war stories.

It should feel calm, business-like, and respectful.

Your body language needs to say:
"This is how professionals work."

Opening part two:
This time, open seated.

A grounded opening works best:

"Earlier, I spoke about trust and about my commitment to making your jobs easier and more productive. As you know, I've spent a little time in the field, spoken with a few customers, and begun to understand how this business really operates day-to-day.

Today is about agreeing how we work together, what standards matter, and how we measure success – fairly, consistently, and transparently."

Then stop.
Let it land.

Standards – not rules:
Avoid the word rules.
Rules feel imposed.
Standards feel professional.

You are not inventing standards – you are codifying what good already looks like.

This meeting should clearly define expectations around:

- Time and territory management
- Reporting and visibility
- Customer care and internal alignment
- Communication up and down the line

Always frame these as enablers, not constraints.

Accountability – calm but firm:
Now comes the moment many avoid.

Handle it simply.

"Trust works both ways. I will back you when you are honest, professional, and committed. I will not back behaviour that damages customers, colleagues, or the business."

No threats.
No drama.
No raised voice.

Authority doesn't need volume.

Closing your first meeting:
End with direction, not inspiration.

"From here, my focus will be one-to-one time with each of you. I want to understand what you need to succeed and where I can remove friction. What we've discussed today sets the baseline. What we do next builds the future."

Thank them. Mean it – and then on to other business if such is required.

Farewells should come with a final handshake for all.

Working with The Sales Office

Here we will be looking at the two basic scenarios:

The Sales Office is not under your direct control.

The Sales Office is under your direct control.

Working without Direct Control

Hopefully you've already had a brief introduction on day one. So, if you do not have direct responsibility for the internal sales office, influencing their output can be a little tricky. They all need to know you, trust you and like you if they are going to be a real asset to you. To achieve this, they need to understand that they will be working 'with you' – and you with them, to maximise the sales potential of the business.

Getting close:
You need to build rapport, both with each team member and their direct supervisor or manager – and therein lies the key. If you don't have direct control of sales office activity, the reason is more than likely that company 'structure' classes the staff in that office as 'Administrators', not sales people. Their function is to deal with orders and take phone calls.

You may be surprised to find that this team is pretty low-key in terms of their actual sales ability. They have zero intention of maximising the sales potential that their contact with the customer can bring. Many are employed purely for their office admin skills rather than sales ability.

It can often be the case that their actual 'people skills', let alone their sales skills, are never explored at interview and not really demanded beyond a vague understanding to be polite whenever possible. They are in fact employed as 'trouble-shooters' and 'order takers' not 'order makers'.

If this is the case, you have a cultural hill to climb, and, as mentioned above, the initial key to change here is your relationship with that office supervisor/manager and indeed the company's understanding of just what a difference such an office can make to profitability if the staff are trained to present 'this month's offer' or even just suggest an add-on to a purchase just made.

Think about it for a moment. One operative taking just ten calls a day has well over 2,000 opportunities a year to increase sales! Five in the sales office represents 10,000 such opportunities, and a 10% success rate = 1,000 additional sales a year.

SURPRISE!

You may also have another surprise in store: That any suggestion you make about teaching sales office staff to 'sell', could be greeted with something between disdain and outright laughter – followed by the claim: *"We don't have time for all that, we have paperwork to do!"* If this is the case, then you definitely have your work cut out.

Then, dare I add, the sales force may hate the idea too – claiming such an initiative would cost them sales and commissions – you'd be taking food out of their kids mouths!

WOW!

My answer?: 'Well ... best make sure your customer never has a need to call the office then, that he's well stocked at all times and that he has your contact details easily at hand!'

Encouraging change:
So, the first step is to develop as positive a relationship as you possibly can with both the staff and their management. Talk, too, with your own senior management about the wasted opportunity in additional

sales that the sales office currently represents. Why not offer the sales office staff incentives to ask for an order: "Would you like an X with that Y, they're on offer this week?" Simple!

If the sales office manager reports to the financial director or some other party, you need to encourage change. The current overseer may not be in favour because you are suggesting reducing their power base while increasing your own, given that, it may never happen – but that shouldn't prevent you from diplomatically making the case.

But, if having control of the sales office is a non-starter and you're stuck with the status quo, what is Plan B?

Plan B:
Firstly, keep an ear to the ground. Listen whenever possible when calls are being handled. Listen to customer feedback about their treatment when calling in, because the absolute basic need is for politeness and diplomacy at all times and if it's not happening, this at least, needs to be addressed. Sales office staff can be poor at this and accounts department staff – even worse.

Next, work toward making sure your sales force is befriending the sales office staff. It's rarely the case that they're not, because they know, being the smooth-talking types that they are, that this is the best way to get things done.

Get the sales office staff close to the customers. Whenever a customer visits the company for whatever reason, a tour, a meeting, a collection, etc., try to get them to spend a moment in the sales office, shaking hands, saying hello, facing never-before-seen, in many cases putting names to voices – because names are rarely offered.

Getting them close:
Critically, in relation to the sales office staff's relationship with customers, work hard with all concerned to encourage the use of their names when taking orders, dealing with queries or promising to help

resolve a problem. This may sound obvious, but it often doesn't happen because the staff don't want that level of commitment to the issue – just in case they forget to follow through! Insisting a name is offered makes such occurrences far less likely.

If you really want to push the boat out and be 'radical', and if you feel company culture is ready for it, arrange for that sales office supervisor/manager to spend a day with a trusted sales exec, out in the field, getting some 'real world experience' and again some one-to-one time with the people who actually pay their salary

Then … hang on to your hat … encourage that manager to let his staff do the same!

Working with Direct Control

Another surprise: Resistance can be subtle. Even if you have full control of the sales office, you still need to tread wisely. This, because between you and the people in direct contact with your customers, is their supervisor or manager.

It is important then, that this situation is handled carefully, because in some cases that management line could attempt to stand between you and much direct contact or influence with the office team. It's almost a tribal leader thing. Some sales office personnel may even encourage their line manager to stand between you and them, afraid, as they may be, of your status or indeed the changes you may want to make.

Meeting the Sales Office Manager:
If at all possible, before you walk into that office, get to know the names of everyone in there. Then arrange a one-to-one with the office supervisor or manager. This will be the equivalent of a 'smart/casual' affair – friendly but purposeful, and should be held uninterrupted.

You need to know that they are on-side with your own thinking about the way things need to be done from here on, but you should not do that by presenting a day-one list of thoughts on the matter. Better by far to use your ears more than your mouth at this first in-depth meeting. You need to begin to understand the prevailing office culture. Ask a lot of questions and carefully note the replies. Here are a few examples:

- How long have you been with the company / in this position?
- Are you happy with the way things work here?
- Do you have plans for future personal development … or …
- Are you happy as you are?
- Talk to me about a typical 'day in the life of Sales Office Manager'.
- Talk to me about the office staff work ethic.
- What do you see as their main duties?
- Are they encouraged to sell?
- Talk to me about each of the individuals in the office:
- Your understanding of their commitment to their work;
- Their ambitions and their likelihood to achieve them within the company.
- Do you feel the office is under staffed /over staffed?
- What changes would you like to see?
- Are there any thoughts or ideas you have presented in the past that were rejected, but that you feel are still relevant to future improvement?

You're trying to get a feel for how well this person 'fits' with your own beliefs about what needs to change and how likely you are to be supported in your endeavours.

Sharing your thoughts:
Finally, share the most relevant (only) of your own thoughts, gleaned from early moments spent with the sales force, with customers and indeed your general beliefs relative to this situation.

Don't present major ideas for change at this first meeting. Give thanks for the time spared and make it clear you will be discussing much of the subjects covered a little further down the line.

– and then – something of a (potential) bomb shell …

An opportunity rarely exercised but so worthwhile.

Meeting the Sales Office Staff – Individually!:
You need to arrange to meet each of the office staff on a one-to-one basis. This needs to take place as soon as possible and should start with the filing clerk and end with the most senior person in that office!

Why not the other way round? Believe me, firstly, it's a great 'leveller' that does much to neutralise 'the pecking order' and also, chances are, if you start at the top, you'll never get to the bottom – other 'urgencies' real or perceived, will get in your way, time passes and it's too late.

At these individual meetings, try to be as informal as possible – it's just a, 'hello, I'd like to get to know you a little before we start working together'. Your main purpose is to judge for yourself each person's work ethic, their responsibilities, their degree of commitment to the company and their ambitions, if any, for their future in the business.

I say 'if any' because some may have serious ambitions that fall outside of the company that may even steal them away – to be a mother, a rock star or world explorer, and it's well worth knowing these things before you get to planning future structure.

These individual meetings done, you need to take a step back and consider what is realistically achievable in the short term and what may be 'doable' a little further down the line.

You need to keep an eye open for 'golden nuggets' within the team – people you feel are both on-board with your style of thinking and ready to help all they can to move the business forward.

You also need to have an eye for 'bad apples', those who will forever undermine anything you may have planned, and believe me, they are very likely to be there.

Sorting the wheat from the chaff:
There's a great deal of clarity that comes from the steps I'm advocating . It's all fundamental steps in critical communication and in this case – the biggest of those steps is dealt with now.

You need to arrange a meeting of all the sales office staff – including those filing clerks and the office manager. All in one room at one time. This will probably be the toughest thing to organise so far, because their presence manning the phones is critical.

Some offices take an hour lunch break and the phones are set to auto response – I don't encourage this, in fact it's something I would encourage you to abolish, but if it's in place right now, perhaps you could arrange a lunch time meeting in the board room with food and drinks laid on. If that's not possible, then a meeting set an hour before the office opens or an hour after it closes or indeed, an early evening meeting in a local hotel, again with some food and drinks laid on.

Communicating your thoughts:
At this meeting you will present your vision of the future as it relates to their everyday lives. You'll talk a little of your experience so far with the sales force, the customers, their management and indeed the time that you have spent with each of them individually.

You need to present a list of things you feel need their attention. That list should be born of your conversations within the company arena so far. Their concerns, customer concerns, sales force concerns, manage-ment concerns and indeed your own concerns about the way things are versus the way you intend for them to be from this day forth.

This includes an accent on: the quality of the service they offer; the speed with which customer issues are resolved; the subject of politeness with which they conduct their business and indeed that 'simple matter' of always offering their name.

If they currently sell as part of their work routine, you will have discussed that before now and perhaps have some plans relating to their future activities in this area.

If they don't currently sell, and you believe they could, draw up plans to train them in the necessary skills and either announce those plans at this meeting or make them aware such plans are in the pipeline.

Add to this missed opportunities for add-on sales, weak complaint handling, or a reluctance to take ownership, and the damage compounds over time.

Offering a name at the beginning and end of a call, listening properly to a problem, and taking responsibility for follow-ups should be routine. Too often, they aren't.

A little-recognised truth that needs to be understood:
The telephone is the greatest magnifier of attitude there is.

Fatigue, frustration, indifference, all travel down a phone line instantly. Customers may empathise, or they may not. Either way, what they experience becomes the company's attitude in their mind.

Closing Out:
With 'any questions?', this should conclude this session with your staff. Telling them you're open their future input. By the end of this meeting, and given your earlier conversations, there should be no doubt in anyone's mind about the direction you will be taking the company and the part you expect your staff to take in helping make things happen.

Given that, any 'bad apples' will already have realised that they are under the magnifying glass. This makes it easier for you to have further, meaningful conversations with them about being part of the solution rather than part of the problem – and it won't take many such conversations before your task of moving them out, if need be, becomes a whole lot easier.

They'll know what's coming before you draw breath to say it.

Hiring & Firing Sales People

Hiring Sales People

The interview arena:

Be sure the arena itself looks clean and professional, be that your office or a hotel suite, etc. Personally, I hate hotel lobby interviews – don't do it. It looks cheap and is not relaxing when you and/or your candidate feel the guy behind is listening to every word!

I'm a great believer in personally greeting candidates at the earliest possible moment. Get out of your office, get into reception, shake hands, welcome them and show them through. Having your secretary or some other staff member bring them to you is pretentious power-play and totally unnecessary in the vast majority of cases.

Interviewing sales people:

Whether what follows applies to your first or your one-hundred-and-first time in the interviewer's chair – listen up. You may think that once you've mastered the techniques that equip you for best practices as an interviewee, that you've pretty-well got what is needed to perform as an interviewer – it's just the same thing from the other side of the desk – right?

WRONG!

Chances are that following the methods used by those who have interviewed you in the past, will serve you very badly. Frankly, most interviewers have never trained for the task, never read any techniques and don't do it for a living! They're flying by the seat of their pants, hoping for the best.

They'll ask a few important questions, get a feel for the chemistry between themselves and the interviewee and make a choice based on who they 'feel' is best – or (worst case) who they think will do an okay job, but just as important to them – someone they think they can control.

Others drop candidates because they see them as a threat to their own position – Not clever! But then, even reading my own earlier thoughts on how to be interviewed successfully, isn't going to give you all the answers either. All such advice is based on getting you through the obstacle course, not about how to build it in the first place!

Now it's your turn to lay out the hoops and see how your candidates perform.

Understanding some basics:
You are interviewing sales people. They're supposed to know how to sell and you don't need them if they are lacking in this area. That's tricky-part number one, because most are pretty good at selling themselves, too, and this to them, is just another sales pitch where reality may be stretched beyond belief.

You need to be mindful of this because you are a sales person, too, and – ironically – most sales people are the easiest people to sell to. It's a phenomenon that I believe is born of empathy for the task and a desire to reward a job (presentation) well done. So you do need to guard against that empathy, too.

What's the harm? Your empathy could be seen as a weakness and/or positive affirmation that 'once in,' they'll be able to play you like a fiddle. But conversely, in many ways, there's nothing wrong with having a little empathy for their task in securing this post unless those thoughts dominate the interview and your decision-making process.

You're not looking for a new best friend, you're looking for the most competent sales person.

So how do you separate the two?

The answer is two-fold:

- Your ability to see through the blarney.
- The filters you use on your applicants.

Breaking through the blarney:
Let's deal with the blarney first. Here, to a great extent, I have to put the onus on your own ability to delve a little deeper when a proud boast is claimed. Don't be afraid to challenge such statements – not doing so can have a profound effect on your relations with this person should you decide to hire them. Firstly, because they will be of the opinion that you are easily 'taken in', and secondly because they are likely to be a disappointment on the job.

Here are a few examples of how to seek substance:

"I have been top of sales for each of the last three years!"
"Really. That's impressive. Can you show me that on paper?"

"I've always been a big fan of your company."
"That's nice, so what's your favourite product / service element?"

"Joe Key-account is a personal friend!"
"Really. That's good to know. I'm meeting him next month, and I can't for the life of me remember his wife's first name – You must know it then?"

Boastful claims are great if interviewee's can substantiate them, not good at all if you can see straight through them.

Order of play and filtering out the good guys:
A few niceties of course: How was your journey? Did you find us okay? etc.

Ask the candidate for their understanding of the vacancy. The answer will offer lots of clues about the level of interest being shown and the amount of research that's been done and their commitment to securing this post.

Getting down to business:
This is where my own recommended method is markedly different to most. It's very simple, highly effective and will support your on-going efforts to monitor both this new member of your team and indeed, as will be shown later, the current sales force, too.

So here goes …

At this point I present two letter-size sheets of paper and say this:

"Here I have two lists. One is a bullet point list of the job I need doing and the other, a bullet point list of the perfect person to do the job.

Now, let me assure you before we start discussing this second list: I am not this perfect person and I haven't met anyone else that is – so if you offer me a 100% thumbs up to every item on here, I'm not likely to believe you! Okay … so let's start with the job I need done …"

Quite obviously, this list will vary dramatically from one industry to another and one company to another, and so it will need some work on your part to hone what follows to suit your own needs.

From time-to-time the lines may be blurred between these lists, you may feel an item I've put on one list would be better placed on the other. Within reason it doesn't matter, what matters is that it's there, it's discussed and it's agreed to be important.

So … be mindful – you're not just reading these lists – you're discussing every bullet point on there until you're satisfied.

So, to add a little meat to the bone, here are a couple of examples:

List One – The job you require done:

- Acquiring an in-depth knowledge of the product/service.
- Knowledge of how to close a sale and how to ask for the add-on.
- To dress appropriate to the trade.
- To be at the first call at 9am (or whatever time your industry dictates)
- An ability to work away from home (exhibitions, vacant territory cover and so on.)
- Courtesy to customers regardless of circumstance.
- Communication skills: Customers, office staff etc.
- A keen administrator: Paperwork carefully completed and in on time.

List Two – The perfect person to do the job:

- Early riser.
- Thoughtful dresser.
- Able to work alone.
- Personable: Gets along with everyone.
- Great Relationship Builder: Customers/Office, etc.
- Persistent: Hard-working. Determined.
- A 'No Quit' attitude until the end of the day.
- Excellent verbal presentation skills.
- A good memory for product names, prices and model numbers, etc.
- A great closer: Ask for three favourite closing statements.
- A good administrator: Orders in on time. Completing reports, etc.
- Healthy – A good health record.
- Safe Driver: Ask about recent accidents, endorsements, pending litigation, etc.

That's not an exhaustive list, but as indicated, it has to be what you want or expect, so set about building both lists – soon – even if you don't aim to interview in the near future – I'll tell you why shortly.

If used judiciously, these two lists will tease out all manner of important information – and that's without any of the 'tough interview questions' we dealt with earlier. So let's cover that, now that you're the interviewer.

Those tough interview questions:
My best advice on tough interview questions: Keep them relevant and go easy. Yes, it's good to put your candidate on the spot occasionally; it helps you see how they cope under a little pressure. It can tease out both strengths and weakness – but they are not the be-all and end-all of great interview techniques. They're a tool, often over-used by less savvy interviewers.

Back then, you needed to be aware of them because stumbling could cost you a job, but now is no time for 'revenge', it's time to reap the best of those questions and let the rest be gone.

Hire for attitude – Train for skill:
Base the majority of what you want to learn from this candidate on their keenness to work with you and their general attitude to people, to life and their achievements, rather than how cleverly they answer tough questions.

Yes, it's important they perform well against the lists above, but it's equally important that they want to give you what they've got, 100% and want to learn the rest.

Closing out the interview:
You need to have decided whether pay and package will be discussed at this interview or later – if later, it does no harm to state that their package will be in line with industry standards and perhaps higher than some.

I once attended an interviewer for a top-flight UK furniture manufacturer, tell me at the end of the interview: "When we disclose your package, it will be non-negotiable. It may be higher or lower than other members of the team – Once hired, discussing your pay with colleagues is a dismissible offence. Seriously.

You may also find your salary doesn't measure up to some others out there, but one thing I can tell you for sure, you will never be happier anywhere else and as you prove your worth, your salary will reflect that."

Hmm!

You need to discuss availability and preferred commencement dates. You need to ask if the candidate would be available/able to attend a second interview in (time frame), and you need to ask if they have any questions for you.

That done, it's another firm handshake and I'd suggest walking them out to their car, talking casually as you go – "How long before you'll be home?", that kind of thing. I'm suggesting the walk out because a cursory look at their car can tell you a lot about a person – remembering they have prepared for this interview. Is the car clean and tidy inside and out? Are any sales materials nicely kept? The sort of things you won't be asking about, but observing.

That's it, interview over. Back to your desk to make the necessary notes … and you're done? Not quite …

One big question you need to ask yourself:
When you're busy considering this candidate with respect to their score out of ten as a sales person – make that score relative to your own sales abilities! Bet that caught you off guard!

Well hang on to your hat because I'm going to do it again. You are only allowed to score your own sales ability as 8/10 … And the killer punch … You're looking for an 8 or a 9 or a 10!

Relax into that thought, because your own abilities go way beyond your ability to close a sale.

Under these rules, most would be looking for a 6 or a 7, but if you want to drive this company forward, everyone on your team needs to be at least as good as you and preferably better – and don't be shy about broadcasting that to your fellow directors!

You will amaze them with the braveness of your statement and be offering proof-positive that it is your marketing skills, your people management skills and general management skills that matter most to the business now. To grow, you need the cream of the crop. "I'm a coach now – and the best coaches are not always the best players!"

One of my all-time favourite sales managers once told me, much to my surprise, that I was a far better salesman than he would ever be – and I was managing his old patch! I was flattered of course, but mostly I admired him for his courage in saying the words. (You know who you are, sir!)

You cannot drive a business upward trying to maximise the potential of second-class players. There are simply not enough carrots or sticks in the world to make it happen!

It's a comfort (sometimes) though, to know that the typical 'hire for subservience' attitude is probably what the sales director in your chief competitor's company is doing, for fear of being seen as inadequate or being ousted by one of his own team. I'd tell my team exactly what I'm looking for and what I expect, adding: "When I move up, I need at least three people ready and waiting to take my place."

Firing Sales People

NOTE: If you enjoy firing people, then you and I can have little in common and this training is probably not for you!

A precursor:
During my early days in sales management I found it somewhere between difficult and impossible to coach salesmen (always men in my own case). Most considered themselves seasoned professionals and, in some cases, were many years older than me. They'd feign listening, even sometime feign agreement, but rarely did they actually learn or practice, let alone truly recognise weaknesses in their planning, administration, presentation and closing skills.

In most cases it wasn't that they were dreadful, but that they couldn't see the opportunities they were missing by not honing skills that I could see would benefit from improvement. So I found myself with members of my sales team who were 'okay' and who it would be impossible to fire for measurable levels of incompetence, but who were not performing to 100% of my expectations or indeed of their own potential.

Appraisal made easy:
I hate firing people, yet I have done so many times. The best I can do is to make the process as easy as possible for both parties. Given that, I decided to press harder for change and for my teamster to acquire a basic understanding of what was required.

Initially, my intention was to create a coherent blueprint for appraisal success. Something I could easily discuss with individuals or in group sessions – and with it, life would surely become much easier.

As a sales guy, I always hated 'Appraisal Forms' and appraisal sessions. A long list of boxes required their ticks and crosses and somehow you achieved an aggregate score of just how good or bad you are/were today, complete with a copy to take home and mull over.

Yes, it works – kinda – but it has a draconian, strictly formal feel to it.

The end result of my own labours then, was of course those two interview lists detailed above – a simple affirmation of intent and a declaration of purpose that can be easily and constantly understood. No monthly appraisal forms, with their accompanying flow charts, no mission statement to memorise, and no misunderstanding of what was required.

They know when it's time to go:
It worked with sales team members new and old, because I was able to say, for example: "At the interview, (or the last time we were together) we discussed (whatever aspect concerned me), well from where I'm standing it appears to be something we still need to work on."

After hearing that two or three times about the same subject area, many realise it's simply never going to happen and leave! And for others, you can bet, they know before I drew breath to say it, that it just wasn't working and I'm going to have to let them go.

Communication is key:
I read somewhere many years ago that if you asked the average manager to write down the ten most important functions that his secretary should perform and asked the secretary to do the same – they would produce two different lists! Which is why many-a-person gets fired for incompetence despite believing they were doing a great job!

My lists and the implementation of them assures that this simply cannot happen because everyone knows exactly what's required of them.

You'll find more about the critical role in Part Two under the heading, *Communication is Key.*

Broadening Your Horizons

So far, we've focused on what it takes to step into the role of Sales Director – from assessing your own readiness, through the interview process, and into the early responsibility of aligning and leading the team around you.

Now the lens widens.

It's time to look beyond the sales function itself and consider your influence on promotion, product and service strategy, company culture, and the broader decisions that shape momentum across the business. This is where the role begins to move from managing outcomes to shaping direction – and where your impact can extend far beyond the numbers.

Marketing

In many companies, marketing is a part of the sales directors function, but many sales people – even seasoned professionals who have never had cause to delve into it, have asked me the question:

"What's the difference between Sales and Marketing?" So here goes:

Marketing fundamentals:
Setting out your market stall. Before you can sell anything, you need something to sell, somewhere to sell it and ways to let potential buyers know you have something they can't live another day without, and exactly where to get it.

All of that is marketing: Product research, development, pre-launch testing, advertising and then the hand-over for promotion. Marketing creates demand, sales converts it.

For new ventures, this will begin with considering what the company is going to offer by way of product or service – or both. If you're joining an established organisation, this is already done – but is that changing? Does it need to change? If so, how?

Design:
Being as sure as you can that the like of shape, size, colour and performance are in line with – or better – exceed, market needs and desirability.

Testing:
Presenting prototypes and potential sales campaigns to end-users and asking their views.

Here, you're not asking, 'Will this sell?', you're asking, 'Would you buy it?' There's a huge difference – it's easy for potential buyers to say, 'I can see a market for that,' without the precursor, 'I don't want or need it myself, but …'

You're looking for positive affirmation, not generalisation. Ten out of ten may be happy to tell you, 'You're going to make a fortune with that', only for you to find on launch, they don't buy it!

Testing price is important, too. Here you may want to offer bracketed examples that give you wiggle room down the line.

Who are you selling to?:
Decide you target profile. You're looking for a 'niche' not a cover-all. There's an old adage still as true as ever: 'A product made for all, is a product made for none.'

In essence that means, if it fits every market, it's going to lack the individuality that makes it stand out from the crowd. As such, quality will without doubt be compromised to satisfy all budgets, competitors will easily move in to out-perform you and then few, if any, will buy.

Branding and promotion:
Company image, logo, sales literature etc., come firmly under the marketing banner. What does your company 'look like' to the world? This one is huge. It's effectively how people view your shop window and not a matter to be taken lightly.

Here, professional help is critical. Unless you're a natural at design, choosing colours, fonts, photography, layouts, and a great deal more, leave it to the pro's and be happy that you know a good thing when you see it.

Advertising – Reaching your target audience:
Here I want to deal with a well-worn business myth: 'The world will beat it's way to the better mouse trap.' Possibly one of the most dangerous 'beliefs' that the business world far too often embraces. It's basic claim being that if you create something exceptional, word will get out and all will come running to your door to buy. No! You need to let the market know what you've got and why they can't live without it.

How do you achieve that? That's a question with a multitude of answers from nurturing word-of-mouth to massively expensive advertising campaigns and sponsorship deals. Common sense dictates much then depends on the organisation's ability to fund such activities, and a carefully organised strategy with an affordable budget that together, best assure a positive return.

As mentioned above, advertising takes on many forms. Your job is to work out what type of advertising your target audience will be warm to and where they are likely to see it, hear it and respond to it.

In conclusion:
My main purpose here is to show you what others may not – not what you can easily find elsewhere. Marketing is a critical business discipline. Your job is not to become a marketer – but to know enough to recognise when marketing is helping sales – and when it's

getting in the way. Thankfully, there are books-a-million specifically on the subject.

Treat yourself, you won't regret it.

In Part Two, under *A Meeting of Minds,* I show how design and presentation can silently undermine even the strongest quality ethic – and sales effort.

Company Culture

Observing it – Changing it:
Boy, this is a big one – and as sales director it's one you may have
more power to nurture, protect, and if necessary, change, than you
may realise.

There's little doubt, you have probably experienced company cultures
in your own life one way or another. Companies that appear to be
little more than a disparate group of individuals, suffering the
consequence of a *'we're no worse than anyone else'* culture.

I can't even see it as a 'decision' that senior management made at
some point and now all on board just live it. It just seems 'to be' –
hanging there over the company like the smell of a rotting carcass
that everyone somehow ignores. A line from a song by 'The Eagles'
comes to mind, It's ... *Like a broken-down carousel, where somebody
left the music on!*

And who's to blame?

Apathy starts at the top:
You look around. Everybody in this business seems to be just 'getting
on with it'. You'll find those who never cared – it's just a job to them.
You'll find those who used to care – but just gave up – and you'll find
what I call, 'The Golden Nuggets'– those who still care and live a life
of frustration trying to get folks to realise there is another way.

There's no doubt in my mind that this kind of problem starts at the
top. A management team with scant regard for the thoughts, feelings
and, heaven forbid, the ideas of those 'beneath them'.

They discourage their department heads from slowing down administration or production for the sake of a little more care. Far better to
do things the way they've always been done – and if an item on its

way out of the door isn't quite up to scratch, let it go – once it's out there it might stick – we'll deal with it if it comes back the other way!

'Give it a run' was a favourite line on the production line of a company I once worked with – but not for long, once I got in there.

How to recognise great culture:
That's easy. There's 'fresh air' about the place. People smile a lot coming to work – not just because they're leaving at the end of the day. People at all levels are not afraid to present new ideas. Managers are listeners. The product or service is well-loved and respected by those who make it, sell it or use it. None of this is accidental.

Changing poor culture:
Change needs people of influence – not necessarily with a title – who have the right mindset. Here I use my 'light bulb' analogy. I've seen companies with great culture where a single person, in the right position drives it. It's a joy to see how that person's presence filters through every corner of the company. They are 'the light' by which all are guided.

Sadly then, they leave this mortal coil or leave for pastures new and someone with a my-way-or-the-highway attitude fills that spot. What happens? – The light goes out – almost instantly.

On the other hand you have a company in the doldrums. The type I described at the beginning of this piece. The new arrival enters with bright ideas, sanctioned by a management team that has no real idea what's wrong; they just know it needs fixing!

The new arrival knows that company culture has never been truly addressed and sets about making change. What happens? The light comes on – but it's like the old fluorescent tubes that flicker a while before offering a steady glow. The new arrival will have ups and downs as will all around them – but with a positive attitude, driven by realistic goals, good things will happen.

You are looking for the opportunity to be that person. Which brings us full circle to my earlier assertion, *'Ability is nothing without opportunity.'* If you're going to enter the management team of a company that is under-performing, be sure that you are going to be allowed to shine.

Making good culture happen:
Maybe surprisingly to some it's incredibly simple – but navigating that simplicity can be a little complex. As someone once said: 'There's nothing more complicated than keeping it simple.' And you can add to that: 'There's nothing common about common sense!'

Having people understand your aims and going along with your plans is where the simplicity and your battle for common sense begins. Getting people on board with your ideas needs proven validation – that what you are advocating actually works and will make a difference.

So let's deal with that:

It's simple – lead by example.

Here, it's not just good to sweat the small stuff – it's critical.

Everywhere you go, everyone you speak with, make people feel good about what they do. Praise them, take an interest in them and what they do, nurture them. Make them aware of how important their function is, no matter how small a cog they may be in the machine. Show them where something that's a part of their daily routine could be done a little differently and how doing so would help the business run more smoothly, and how good that would make them feel about themselves and the tasks they perform.

Handle mistakes calmly. Don't play the blame game, work with people to find solutions. It's how you speak, how you listen, how you set the tone. Before long you find people do start to feel better about themselves and the tasks they perform and will actually start to mimic your own behaviour – smiling more, being kinder to those around them, helping out where they can – the culture is now beginning to grow.

Get close to those who have any part in the quality of the product or service the company offers. Encourage them away from the 'good enough' attitude to a place where they become proud of their role in helping make things better. Be consistent and those around you will want to be consistent too.

Every area where you see small changes will polish those rough edges – dive in, make good things happen in small ways and when the time comes to tackle the big stuff, those around you will believe in you, stand behind you and want to get it done.

Leap-frogging the front line – not good!:
It doesn't work … but 'corporate' very often can't see that – because they're AWOL when it matters.

I smile when I see evidence of large corporations masking poor culture behind fanciful statements. Statements that are there to supposedly impress the workforce or the customers or both.

Mission statements, forged in hallowed halls that senior management demand are filtered down to all on board. They issue these over-blown statements and then get back to their ivory tower or the golf course, as soon as they can. They've announced what's expected, with a directive to either conform or be fired! False threats and draconianism at work again.

I was once irritated by a young lady at a supermarket checkout, who, while pushing through my substantial cartload, was far too busy chatting with a co-worker at the next station to be bothered acknowledging me at all. Once done, I couldn't help but lean in as I left to say calmly, "Thank you, might be nice."

Her rely? Frightening:

"It's on the receipt!"

Sure enough, there it was the final line – put there by corporate who knew full well their operatives wouldn't be bothered to say it. So these days, when I exit a business and see a sign that reads, "Thank you, please call again soon." I know very well why it's there.

The long-term cost of cultural drift is explored further in Part Two, particularly in *The Loss of a Brand* and *Greed or Flailing Desperation.*

Delegation

It won't be long before you will need to delegate some tasks to others, be that a one-off, temporary, or permanently. If you're uncomfortable with that thought, you'll need to take a few deep breaths, seek out trusted colleagues and let go.

Things you should not delegate:
Disciplinary issues, strategic decisions, anything requiring authority, and tasks with high risks if done incorrectly.

So, I'm not talking about major tasks, but some of the mundane that stack up quickly and bog you down just as fast. It's so easy to think, 'It will be done quicker if I do it myself. I don't need other people's mistakes frustrating me.' These are understandable concerns. What are not – and should never stop you delegating are thoughts such as, 'I'll lose control,' or 'I don't want to burden people.'

If you sweat this kind of small stuff, you will burn yourself out and achieve precious little.

Think of it this way: True delegation helps bring structure, helps others feel supported – knowing they are helping. You're not 'dumping' on others in a 'just sort it out' fashion. The tasks you let go add to the recipient's capabilities, to their job description, to their very security – they have something to take ownership of. They see themselves as ever-more needed and that feels good.

Who to trust:
Starting early, keep an eye open for those who are consistent, reliable, organised, willing, calm under pressure and open to feedback.

How to delegate:
Make it clear what the purpose of the delegated task will be. If there's a deadline, be very sure this is clearly understood. Point the recipient in the right direction for resources.

Review the outcome: Praise progress, refine the process.

Build confidence by explaining why they were chosen. Agree on check-in's where necessary. Not in a 'micromanagement' way, but often enough to retain momentum.

Offer support – make yourself available but not intrusive.

Delegation works best with clear standards, follow-though and trust.

A golden rule of delegation:
Delegate the task – not the responsibility for the results! A job can be well done even if the outcome isn't all you would have expected. The task can be completed exactly to plan, but outside factors can affect results. Important to always remember here: they are responsible for execution of the tasks you set, you stay accountable for the outcome.

Things to consider delegating:
Routine administrative tasks, research and preparation, follow-ups, elements of larger projects.

A common delegation error:
Delegating too much, too early. Feel the 'weight' of the task for yourself, understand it. Know what it takes to see it through successfully.

Taking tasks back at the first sign of a problem:
Discuss the issue. See how well your appointee is coping. Compliment them. Coach them. 'Let's look at what happened and why. What got in the way? Were any steps unclear? How can I best support you?'

Resolve the issue together and offer praise where they offer solutions or help significantly to that end. Fix the process not the person.

The delegation mindset:
Let go of the task, but hold firmly to the standard. You remain the guardian of quality, timeliness, professionalism – and the outcome. Your team becomes a well-oiled engine that delivers the work.

When you master delegation, your workload lightens, your team grows, stress reduces and performance strengthens.

Time Management

Managing it, protecting it and using it wisely:
Time is your sharpest tool, your scarcest resource and your greatest asset – if you learn to protect it.

Time is the currency of good leadership:
You spend it well, you lead well. You spend it poorly and you drown in noise, stress and exhaustion.

The big myths of time:
I don't have enough of it. I must be available to everyone. If I work harder, I'll catch up. Everything is important – I must be there.

The three tenets of leadership time

1: High-Value Leadership Time:
Planning. Strategy. Coaching. Systems. Decision-making.

2: Supportive Time Management:
Check-ins. Admin. Reviewing (Meaningful) Reports.

3: Being Alert to the Time Thieves:
Interruptions. Firefighting. Vague meetings. Unnecessary admin. Emotional noise. Doing the work of others.

Setting boundaries
People are very good at off-loading their problems on others and then walking away. Don't be one of their targets! Get used to treasuring your time. Be the champion of your own time.

You've probably been told yourself, from time-to-time, 'Not now,' by your senior management and others. That's not discourtesy when offered with respect – it's how it sometimes has to be.

Don't be shy about offering responses such as:

- "I can't deal with that right now – let's schedule it."
- "Can you speak to X about this first?"
- "Let me come back to you at 3pm."
- "Send me the outline of that before we meet."
- "I think I can trust you to deal with that."
- … and so on.

Don't be afraid to bat the ball back in their court, even if only temporarily – when the time is right – for you.

Going Deep:
This is an essential. Great artists and writers must 'go deep' to create their best work. It's 'time out' of sorts, but it's deeper than that.

It's almost meditative in nature. It's digging deep into your consciousness to bring out the best.

Well, great managers 'go deep', too. It's imperative. You can't be the 'creative' you need to be with all the hustle and bustle going on around you.

You need at least one hour of quality, 'alone-time' every day!:
No calls — No emails — No meetings — No interruptions.

This is your time to think, plan, solve problems, write and review. The results will be measurable.

Back to work and – more time killers:

Firefighting:
It feels urgent, even heroic, but it's born of weakness. Root it out, stamp it out.

Oh, those meetings:
Many meetings are calendar driven. Folks scramble for something to contribute because it's the regular, 'third Thursday of the month' meeting. Consequence? The meetings are usually, too long, too vague, and unnecessary.

Rules and Boundaries:
If there's no meaningful agenda – there's no meeting.
If you're not needed – and I mean *needed*, don't attend.
Keep your own meeting purposeful, structured and brief.

Emails – messages – written noise!:
Check emails twice daily. Don't reply instantly unless urgent. Delegate responses when possible. Make it known that you'd prefer issues 'bundled' – No drip-feeds.

How to prioritise – a critical list:
Value what comes from, or contributes to:

- Strengthening your team.
- Improving systems.
- Encourages clear communication.
- Solving root problems.
- Supporting planning.
- Supporting performance.
- Enhances quality.
- Enhances customer service.

Protect yourself from burnout:
Be aware that burnout is fuelled by: Constant interruptions, unclear priorities and boundaries, emotional overload, carrying the team alone.

Prevent it with: clarity, structure, rest, delegation, saying no, asking for support – going deep! – It *really* matters!

Conclusion:
Time is something great leaders actively defend. When you protect your time, your judgment sharpens, your leadership strengthens, your team flourishes.

There's an old Zen saying that's noteworthy:

'Spend twenty minutes in nature every day, unless you're busy, then spend an hour.'

I'll leave you with that thought.

Communication is Key

Practice 'Interpretive listening' by seeking out the meaning beneath the words. Listen for patterns, problems, early warning signs, emotional under-currents and opportunities.

Communicating instructions:
What needs to be done

- Why it matters
- How it should be approached
- By when it must be completed

Then ask, 'What questions do you have?'

Communicating bad news:
State it clearly. Be honest – not brutal. Explain the reason. Clarify next steps. Offer support.

Digital communication:
Keep emails short, purposeful and where needed, deadline specific. Don't allow messaging apps to become complaint zones, distractions or drip feeds of low-grade information.

Public speaking, meetings and briefings:
There are books-a-billion out there on public speaking, and my own 'nutshell' thoughts are covered in the segment dealing with your first sales meeting. But if you need the quickest of summaries under this heading, here goes:

Remember to breath – Push all air out to maximise fresh air in.

Structure beats charisma – be clear what needs to be said. Open with purpose. Speak slowly. Keep structure tight. Use simple language. Summarise clearly. Confirm next steps.

Conclusion:

Your communication skills become your reputation, your presence, your authority and your influence – it's leadership in motion.

Authors Notes

Before We Go Further

Everything that follows was learned the hard way.

Not in classrooms. Not in seminars. Not from theory that sounds convincing but collapses under pressure. What does follow comes from years spent in the sales trenches – making decisions with consequences, navigating failure as well as success, and learning what actually works when reputations, livelihoods, and results are on the line.

I didn't enter sales with certified credentials, or a polished career path. What I did have was real–life personal responsibilities – and a need to make things happen. That pressure became a teacher. It exposed weaknesses quickly, punished ignorance without mercy, and rewarded clarity, preparation, and resolve.

Patterns emerged. Some lessons repeated themselves regardless of company, market, or product. Others revealed themselves only after costly mistakes – mine included. Together, they shaped not just how I sold, but how I led, how I built teams, and how I judged readiness for responsibility.

These are truths earned in the trenches.

**Use them to move faster, stand firmer, and
arrive better prepared for your future.**

PART TWO

LESSONS LEARNED
THE HARD WAY

Stories from the field that reveal what theory
never teaches — and experience never forgets.

Truths earned in the trenches

Power to The People

The People Business

Reps, managers, directors, CEOs to work-a-day operatives … it's all the same. Without your people on your side, it's game over.

Serious influences you may never consider:
I once asked a 'trouble-maker' who worked on a factory floor why he picked so many fights with senior management, even though he knew he would rarely win. In a nutshell, his response was: *"It's not about winning or losing, it's about playing the game!"*

This was a friend of a friend I'd converse with occasionally over a pint, and his attitude to working life fascinated me. He was a disrupter. He got his kicks from making sure management didn't get all their own way. He'd work to slow things down, to be as sure as he could that management would fail to reach their goals – and hopefully get them fired!

Why?:
Because he hated them for their stuck-up ways. For always presuming they knew best, and for demanding things were done their way.

The learning curve:
When I was a young lad, sweeping wet sawdust around a wholesale hardware warehouse, I'd observe the sales guys and how they worked with their customers. It interested me how many customers would browse the shelves, effectively waiting in line for Harry – why?

Because more than the others, in this mundane working environment, you could see that Harry cared about the product line and, most particularly, the customers – as individuals. He served them weekly. He knew their names, their wives' names, their company names, and where their stores were. In short, he was a people person.

Later, when I left to become a junior sales guy in an up-market retail furniture store – where you'd typically only see the same customer once a year or so – one member of the sales team had much the same ability to connect with customers. For years afterwards, I would be asked by people I'd never seen before whether Frank was still around.

Putting two and two together very quickly, I decided that although I was introvert by nature, I had to adopt the same principle if I was to be as successful as possible. It worked – and I began to enjoy the connection.

Even later, when selling to pubs and clubs from a van, I found that customers favoured me over other suppliers of much the same product – in this case, I was selling something as unremarkable as common-old meat pies!

So it didn't take me long to realise that selling is the people business, and that stood me in good stead for many a long year.

But in reality, it's even bigger than that.

Over time, those lessons taught me something more profound:

The whole darn shooting-match is The People Business.

Much later in my working life, when I was hired as sales director in a company that was not performing to its best, I encountered the kind of obstructive behaviour outlined at the head of this piece – and realised just how commonplace 'disrupters' were.

The production director knew that the workflow was part of the problem and set about reconfiguring the factory floor, hoping to push more product out faster. He proudly showed me his newly-drawn plans to move heavy machinery around to create a new flow-line. I asked whether he had consulted the various foremen and line workers for their thoughts.

He laughed and replied:

"What the hell do they know, beyond their own little department?"

Being very conscious of 'management boundaries' in this rather draconian organisation, I let it go – almost.

I had already made it my business to walk the factory floor whenever I was there, saying hello to the workforce and checking that urgent orders were being processed with all due speed – well, that was my excuse anyway.

In reality, I wanted to get close. To know at least the names of the foremen, so that during factory tours with retailers I could introduce buyers to the people who actually made and dispatched the product – and conversely, introduce the workforce to those who actually sold what they created. Not me or my sales force, but the people at the sharp end, out there in retail stores.

So I went down for a quiet chat with a couple of these guys and asked whether they had ever thought about improvements to the workflow. All said they knew exactly what needed to be done – but they weren't paid for their ideas; they were paid to do as they were told.

One also mentioned that the production director had recently shown him the new project plan – not to ask for input, but to schedule when the changes would be made. The foreman said:

"I looked at the plan and chuckled inside … no way was his master plan going to make a difference, and no way was I ever going to tell him so!"

Making it right:
Management's number one priority – no matter the level or department – is to get everybody on side. To stretch the boundaries of their

influence as far as possible beyond their own domain, at least to every department that touches there own.

In the exceptional book, *In Search of Excellence* by Tom Peters and Robert Waterman, they credit the phrase 'Management By Wandering Around' (MBWA) to Ed Carlson, then of United Airlines, and later of the Carlson Leadership and Public Service Center.

MBWA can be tougher than it first appears. Simply 'wandering' can be daunting amidst a sea of suspicious faces, all initially convinced you're just another one of 'them upstairs' in a new, 'friendlier' guise.

But over time, building trust – asking questions without rushing to offer answers – will give you a far deeper understanding of what's really going on in the company that you've offered your working life to.

Lessons Never Learned in The Boardroom.

Work hard to get those who make the product, as close as possible to those who sell it. Take that to the bank.

And truths from the ground floor are not limited to deliberate disruptors. The workforce can scupper progress without even realising they're doing it. Look for those weak spots – and work to heal them.

A home-spun truth from me:
The first person I alerted to this situation was the owner of the business. When I explained what I had learned about a particular issue, he challenged me by saying:

"Well that's not what I've heard!"

My reply:

"You have to realise that one of the 'privileges' of managing directorship is that people are likely to tell you what they think you want to hear."

Breaking that mould will bring rewards the like of which are a true joy to experience.

Conversely – And Critically:
If you take the incredibly important step of wandering around the business and talking to people, you will find there are those, in many tears of responsibility, who care deeply about the business and the job they do.

Spending quality time with such folks is worth its weight in gold. Talk to them. More important, *listen* to them. The reward will be paid with insights you will rarely, if ever, encounter in the board room.

Putting Your Sales Force on a Pedestal

The battle against routine derision:
There have been many times during my working life – at all levels within the sales arena – that I have become incredibly frustrated with management's attitudes toward their sales force.

"What's so special about these guys? Anyone can sell stuff – what makes them so important?"
Of course, it's simply not true that anyone can sell stuff, though it is true that most people can take orders from a needy customer.

"Why do we have to pay these guys commission to get them to do what we already pay them for?"
Fact is: We don't pay them what they're worth – they earn their worth.

Love this one – usually asked by those in accounting positions:
"I see Joe had another blank day yesterday – no doubt he stayed home!"
Wow! is about the best I can come up with on that one.

I doubt I need to offer more – you get the drift, I'm sure.

In reality, the sales force are the heartbeat of your company. Without them pumping away at their order books, it all comes to a very nasty halt. Yes, it's critical that you choose the right people – but that done, it is equally critical that they know they are appreciated and rewarded well for their achievements.

Getting it right can be demonstrated in many ways …

Here's a great expression of appreciation that I encountered when arriving at head office for a final interview with a company I would later work with as a self-employed sales associate. While walking the corridors, one wood-framed phrase appeared down the halls over and over again. Its message: *"This company exists because of its salesmen!"* Remember that the entire sales force was actually self-employed.

And so to the simple stuff:
To start with, achievement recognition can be as simple as a sincere pat on the back – with the accent on sincere. Patronising rhetoric is more likely to make the recipient feel ill than appreciated.

But you can do better than that:
It's wise to structure sales force salaries so that around four-fifths of their basic needs are met and the remainder earned through commissions, bonuses, etc. This way, they feel secure – but still motivated. And if a sales person out-performs target levels, everybody wins.

But it can easily get better still:
Many sales people get a kick out of being the 'top performer', but there can only ever be one. Top three works quite well in larger teams, but it still leaves the majority out in the cold – particularly those who feel they can never out-perform Mr. Perfect.

Note: Very careful attention needs to be paid to how 'top performance' is calculated – more on this in the *Meaningful Reporting* section a little further down the line.

I believe it pays to create person-specific targets, with bonuses attached to goals set for that individual alone.

It also pays to monitor performance closely to ensure that opportunities are not being missed simply because the individual doesn't see them.

Then ... how about this:
Have those top performers stand up at sales meetings – not just to receive praise, but to share exactly how they achieved their goals.

Give them plenty of notice to prepare. Otherwise, you'll get anything from silence to garbled bluster because, quite honestly, many winners have never really analysed how they succeed. They just do.

Widening the circle of influence – dare to involve their family!:
For this, I must give full credit to the National Chemsearch (UK) Ltd of the 1970s. I have no idea whether the company still operates under the same philosophy, but back then – they blew my mind.

Let me plant a couple of stakes in the ground first:

1. I was working with them as a self-employed associate, as were all 70+ members of their UK sales force.

2. I had never felt so close, so necessary, or so genuinely appreciated by a company as I was by this organisation back then.

I had been tested through a gruelling first interview. I get the job. I'm about to start selling expensive, high-grade industrial chemical products – cleaners, lubricants, and the like – to maintenance engineers and industrial buyers, within a strictly defined territory.

Day one – I'm collected from home by my Area Sales Manager, who will be with me for a full week of initial product and sales training. A great day, travelling around Stoke-on-Trent in Staffordshire, watching a true professional sell to folks from salt-of-the-earth mechanics to big-brand buyers at the like of Royal Doulton.

The man earned me good money on day one. I was impressed. But not half as impressed as I was when we arrived home to my wife – beaming – greeting my new boss, who had arranged for her to receive a huge bouquet of flowers with a simple message:

"Welcome to the Chemsearch Family! — Jim."

But it didn't stop there. Jim would send her a letter with an 8"×10" photo of, say, a pair of Waterford Crystal decanters, saying:

"Look what John can win for you! All he needs to do is write 20 orders next month – no matter their value – and these beautiful decanters will be yours!"

Now I' have two bosses!

Why did this work so well?

Partly because Jim now had someone pushing me out the door each morning – and questioning my success on return. Partly because those orders couldn't be manipulated. They had to be 20 orders to different companies, and buyers wouldn't split orders due to volume-based pricing. And of course, being self-employed, I wanted every order to count – to maximise commissions.

Clever.

And it went further still:
The company held quarterly conferences – a story all of its own – and once a year they hosted a two-day 'Ladies Conference', inviting wives to a top-class hotel in a prime location, such as Stratford-upon-Avon.

While we were in conference, the ladies enjoyed a day trip, joined us for evening dinners, and stayed overnight – all laid on.

So why did I move on?:
After several successful years with top sales awards, helping train new recruits and enjoying the fruits of success – life intervened. During the coal miners' strike of the early 1970s, the Government imposed a compulsory three-day working week to conserve fuel and power.

Industry slowed to a crawl. Factories closed two days a week. Petrol rationing cards were distributed to every driving licence-holder nation-wide.

For a self-employed salesman, the impact was immediate and brutal. Sales fell by more than 40% instantly. Budgets were slashed as companies focused on survival. With a wife, three young children, a mortgage – and with no clear end in sight– continuing was no longer realistic.

My mantra in those years was simple: *"If I don't sell, my kids don't eat."* With genuine regret, another way forward had to be found.

Getting Close to Your Team

I held the post of Sales Director for a division within a major UK furniture manufacturing group. Mine wasn't the largest division, but its growth had been the highest in percentage terms during my first year.

This piqued the interest of my boss, the Group Marketing & Sales Director, to the extent that – for the first time – he told me he would be attending my next sales meeting. Remarkable to me, by the way, that he told me rather than asked me, and that he had not attended any of my previous meetings.

So he arrives, and when the moment came to settle down to business, he did no more than take a chair and sit himself in a far corner of the room where he pulled out a clipboard and pen. He said nothing during the meeting, but afterwards a critical part of our conversation went like this:

Him: "John… a word."
Me: "Of course."
Him: "An observation."
Me: "Okay."
Him: "Regarding your relationship with the sales force here…"
Me: "Okay."
Him: "I couldn't help but notice that you appear to be… well… only one step removed from your men. I think you need to work on that."

Me: "I see… and would you mind if I made an observation?"
Him: "Of course," he replied – almost stepping backward at my audacity.

I then named the sales director of the largest division in the group. He had been close to this man longer than their tenure at this organisation and they held each other in high esteem. (Ironically, the two had previously worked together at one of the country's top brands – and had bankrupted the business in the process.)

Him: "Yes!" he replied proudly at the sound of the name.
Me: "Well, the fact is, I see him as three steps removed from his sales force."
Him: "Yes!" he replied again – even more peacock-like, sure now that he had made his point.
Me: "Well, the fact is, I see how much his sales force dislike and distrust him. He'll never learn anything from them that isn't offered in the hope of undermining him at least – and unseating him at best.

"Given that, I think you need to understand how hard I'm working to retain my own position. These people know and respect me. They tell me what I need to know, and I act on it where I feel appropriate. It's a big part of why we're performing as well as we are – and I have no intention of distancing myself from them at all."

Our conversation ended not long after that. My thoughts went in one ear and straight out the other, and I'm sure my 'real-world' performance was the only thing preventing him from sacking me for my impudence on more than one such occasion.

That entire group went down two years later, taking my golden-nugget division with it.

In conclusion:
Garner the respect of your sales force and stay close. It's an awful lot tougher than draconianism – but it pays in spades.

Distance may look like authority from the boardroom – but proximity is where real leadership, intelligence, and performance are forged.

Key 'Shut Up' Moments
For Your Sales Force

Sales people love to talk, but there are times when silence is golden. If you've read Part One, you'll know I'm a great believer in having my sales people talk – but there are times out there when they really do need to learn how to shut up!

During a sales presentation:
Do they shut up occasionally? Some dive in, reasonably confident they can answer any 'objections' they hear – and if they're smart, they may even be intuitive enough to hear the silent/hidden objections and navigate their way toward a sale.

But did they take the moments to shut up and listen? Have they 'qualified' the need for the product or service they are selling? Did they ask what the buyer's needs were and then shut up and listen before coaching their offer toward fulfilling that need?

Did they shut up long enough after asking leading questions and give the buyer time to express their thoughts? But even if the answer to these questions is yes, there is one key shut up moment that many sales people seem utterly incapable of practicing …

Ask a closing question and then, *shut up!*:
It's tough, almost nerve-wracking sometimes. The pause could last ten seconds or more than a minute – but the truth of it is … he who speaks first – looses!

An example: Let's say, "So will it be the red or the green?" … A few seconds silence – maybe more – and then the killer: The sales guy can't stand the silence and says, *"The red seems perfect for your needs to me."* And there you have it – something the buyer can disagree with. Something he can say no to. Something that allows him the opportunity to say he needs time to think – maybe because he was thinking, green!

Shut up when the deal is done!:
Another critical moment. After you think the sale is closed, it can be lost in the blink of an eye – it's the incessant habit of continuing to sell after the work is done!

And so to my favourite example:
It came to me via a sales lady I was chatting with about this very subject, and the following was her tale:

She was a young sales assistant on a drapery shop floor. She likened the setting to that of the UK TV comedy show *'Are You Being Served?'*, very posh, very 'traditional'.

The buyer was also the head of sales and on return from a buying trip she presented her latest purchases to her shop-floor staff. One item in particular was an evening gown which was both beautiful and spectacularly expensive.

All of the sales staff agreed that magnificent as the gown was, they would never be able to sell it! Head of Sales was having none of it, and as time went by, she sought to prove that she would find the right customer to purchase it.

Opportunity knocks … Some weeks later, the 'Lady of The Manor' visited the store, looking for something to wear at an annual ball – the perfect target for our Head of Sales – and so she moved in. The rest of the sales team scattered to watch from behind coat racks and mannequins as Head of Sales began her sales pitch.

She spoke much of its beauty and exclusivity and how there was only one of its kind. How well it graced Madam's adorable frame and to seal the deal she added that there was no chance that madam would be caught wearing the same gown as any of the other ladies at the event!

To the silent gasps of the sales ladies around, Madam bit, and with a smug look around at her underlings, Head of Sales escorted The Lady of The Manor to the check out.

Once there she began to wrap the dress, continuing to bestow praises upon Madam for such a wise purchase – how perfect it was for her skin tones, how wonderful she would look, how exquisitely made it was. And then the killer: The final affirmation of just how much Head of Sales agreed with Madam's decision to buy:

"Truth is, Ma-am, I love this dress so much that if you hadn't purchased it today, I'd have bought it myself!"

The response was without hesitation: *"Then you must have it, dear!"* … *"Oh, no-no-no!"* … *"Oh, yes, I insist."*

There was nothing else in the store that took Madam's fancy, and so she left, quite sure she had done the right thing. That dress then hung in the store for years.

One more important example:
Almost equally as often as I experienced these dangerous ramblings, I experienced another 'Don't know when to shut up' phenomenon: sales people seem to forget where the door is.

Hanging around to chat after the sale is closed, is both risky and (I believe) rude. I wouldn't be asking my sales guys to run for the exit and burn rubber in the car park, but there must be respect for the buyer time. Politely leaving soon after the deal is done is a courtesy the buyer will be thankful for – knowing (for example) that the next time this sales person calls, they're not going to be impossible to get rid of.

Making Good Things Happen

Meaningful Reporting

Meaningful reporting came as something of a surprise to a major cabinet furniture manufacturer I worked with as Sales Director.

I managed a team of nine representatives selling across territories all over the UK. On first studying the structure of their sales reporting, one member of the team stood out clearly above the rest. But when I spent time with him in the field, the level of effort he appeared to be putting into the job didn't sit comfortably with his position as the number-one achiever.

Other members of the team appeared far more committed, efficient and effective. Bigger and better retail displays, stronger allegiances from their retailers, closer relationships with buyers and shop-floor sales staff – all the indicators of professionalism were there.

Some of these reps were also high-ranking, but never quite made the cut according to the headline sales statistics, and so a pat on the back for them had been rare.

So I had an idea.

Each sales representative's territory was divided into a number of counties. On paper, the territories looked fairly evenly balanced – but several critical factors were completely off the radar of the company's reporting system. Those factors masked true potential and distorted real performance.

My first question was simple:
How many retailers were there to sell to in the first place – and, just as critically – What size consumer population were those retailers serving?

Sales were 100% UK retailer-based, so crunching some new numbers was actually very straightforward.

My next question:
What was each representative's sales performance per thousand head of population on their territory?

County population data was easy enough to obtain – and then came the 'aha' moment.

My so-called, "Super Star" dropped to third place when assessed against the previous year's sales on a per-capita basis. Meanwhile, my supposed number four performer was actually extracting more business from his territory than anyone else – by a double-digit percentage – and was duly awarded his rightful number-one place.

So beware those headline figures.

They rarely tell the whole story.

Why this matters:
If you reward the wrong numbers, you reinforce the wrong behaviours – and lose your best people. Our previous 'Super-Star' learned he had work to do – much to his own benefit, and that of the company - everybody wins.

Beware the Bean Counters

Pure math is rarely the answer:
Two and two may make five occasionally, but your accountant would much rather it were three.

Those demon discounts!:
This is fair warning to those who may not yet be aware of the potential dangers that lurk within! It's not true in all cases, but I would contend finance rules within well over 50% of larger British and American companies. So you need to be aware of what you may be up against from your financial director and be prepared to fight your corner.

So, for the uninitiated, and with scant apology to any financial directors that may be reading this, let's look at the reality.

Sales want:
Great designs of high quality at unbeatable prices, supported by exceptional service. They also want the best possible cars, plus the best pay and benefits package in the industry.

Accounting wants:
Lowest possible production costs, minimal overhead and highest possible margins.

Production in a nutshell:
Sales want it round – Production (and Accounting) want it square! Your battle to fight.

I remember an MD taking a call while interviewing me and saying, *"Can't talk now, I'm interviewing an overhead."* I couldn't resist mentioning after the call that he was actually interviewing an asset – and maybe that's why I didn't get the job!

To be real – or not to be real – that is the question:
The fact is, the healthiest company cultures are those that celebrate the four most important assets they have:

- their people
- their products
- their quality and service ethic
- and the tireless support of all.

Sadly though, most companies actually believe it's all about those old pretenders to fortune: *volume, price, and profit.* All have their place of course, but it's the degree by which each becomes the company mantra and is pursued at the expense of quality and service support in every area, that can make the difference between mundane performance and even failure or success.

The common belief is that if they aim to produce volume at speed, prices will fall, volume sales will follow and profits will rise. There are truths to that of course, but far too often it becomes the holy grail.

That's a killer philosophy that can be laid firmly at the feet of blind greed by some, and purist accounting by the rest.

You – and the accounts department:
Quite obviously, I'm highlighting these issues because, as a sales director/manager, it's something you need to be fully aware of and can cause major issues as you work to improve the quality of your company's product and the service that supports it.

Accountants have much to answer for in this area. Most see themselves as custodians of the company's funds and often work slavishly to retain every penny earned by ensuring every cost is reduced to a minimum and every price is hiked to the max. Given that, the divide between sales and accounting can be very wide indeed – and when accountants win, the company often loses as a result.

The price you pay:
It starts with raw materials where there's a fine line between volume purchases to reduce costs, or sourcing cheaper alternatives in smaller quantities – or doing both – buying cheap in volume to cut costs yet again!

Then there's cheaper manufacturing equipment and supplies, cheaper packaging materials and distribution costs and of course, cheaper labour. All valid areas for scrutiny, but over-ambitious moves in this direction can have devastating affects on the quality of the product, the morale of the work force and those who deliver the product – then all that spills over to the frustration of the customer who receives a shoddy product often delivered by a driver with 'attitude'.

How to win!

Getting your way by speaking their language:
First of all you agree that keeping a close eye on costs and maximising price are critically important. But then you need to demand – not beg – an understanding that the market will only stand a certain price and that the same market is quality conscious. It's this company's job therefore, to satisfy those needs.

You need them to work with you and find ways to cost-effectively improve quality, increase production, ensure the fastest possible delivery and offer industry-leading support.

Anyone can produce run-of-the-mill merchandise and there are plenty that do – so you have no intention of watching this company produce yet another 'also-ran' product with little better than adequate service support. The way to bulk up that bottom line isn't by mass-producing 'acceptable' merchandise, it's by being the best in your price band or being the best – period.

Responsibility Meets Control

Be sure you actually have control of all you will be responsible for.

It's not always the case.

I was hired as sales director for one division of a huge UK furniture-manufacturing conglomerate with massive brand recognition. The job title, the car, the pay and benefits – all just great.

But I hadn't done many of the things I'm asking you to do.

I took it for granted that all my birthdays had come at once, and boy, was I going to rise through those many-fold corporate ranks in this Big Brand company – and fly!

WRONG!

It didn't take me long to realise that I had no power at all.

By the end of the first week, I had spoken to key customers, gathered my sales force together for a meeting, and begun drawing up my vision for the division's future.

The following week I was called to a meeting at HQ.

There, they presented me with plans they had drawn up for my division – without consulting me at all. Those plans included drastic changes to the product range, to the sales force, and to the office staff – all of which I had *assumed* were under my control.

Few of their proposals made any sense to me and I told them so – clearly, and with reasons.

"Oh no," they ruled.

They had done the research. The marketing department had drawn up the promotional plan. My job, was to sell it to the sales force and get out there with them and make it happen.

The story that followed could be a chapter in its own right, but I'll limit myself to this:

The only time I was ever 'responsible' or 'accountable' for sales performance was at the monthly Directors' Meeting, called by the Group CEO at Head Office, in his key-coded suite.

He had also bestowed upon himself the title of Managing Director of all divisions – though he quite literally never left his ivory tower.

Each division therefore had: A Sales Director, a Production Director and a Financial Director. Do you see the missing component under those various divisional roofs?

No operational leader present. No one person had ultimate control on a daily basis.

Back to that meeting.

No one from this vast group's marketing department ever attended those meetings. Neither did my own boss – the Group Marketing and Sales Director.

And yet, suddenly, it was all down to me.

I was expected to explain:

- Why sales were not all they should be,
- Why their promotions had not succeeded as well as expected,
- Why their targets had not been met – and finally...
- What was *I* going to do about it!

Never, should anyone be asked to take responsibility for anything they do not control.

The net result of this deeply flawed senior management structure? The entire group went down.

The lesson is simple – and critical:
Be absolutely clear about the limits of your authority and influence – and discover them at the first interview, not at the first board meeting.

Accountability without authority is not leadership – it's liability.

Lessons from
an Encyclopedia Salesman

Don't laugh! I sold door-to-door for over a year and often earned four times the average UK income in the process. In my fifty-plus years of selling, this was the best no-can-fail sales presentation I was ever taught.

It was virtually impossible to complete the pitch without success. No pressure. No persuasion. No lies. Just exceptional presentation.

Selling Collier's Encyclopedia:
The folks I was selling to didn't know they wanted – or needed – the product until I knocked at their front door. And it would cost the average couple over two months' pay to buy it.

When successfully concluded, the pitch earned me £20 in commission. Back then (1967–68), that was the average weekly wage.

The point of this story, then, is to walk you through a fail-safe structure – one that salespeople of all would do well to consider.

Here goes…

The Ice-Breaker:
Front door. Clipboard in hand, pilot case at my feet:

"Hi, my name is John. I'm conducting a survey about an educational programme we're introducing into the area and I'm looking for some input from local residents. Would you and your wife/husband be interested in offering your thoughts?"

Yes/No – you're either in, or you're down the road.
Proceed only if both partners are present.

The Relaxers: (Chat)
Do you have kids?
Do you believe in higher education?
Are you looking to improve your own education?
Do you enjoy TV documentaries?
What are your general thoughts on education available in the area?
How far is the local library … that sort of thing.

Positive? Move forward.
Negative? Many thanks – and leave.

Company Presentation:
"Okay. Let me tell you a little about the people I represent."

I would then explain P.F. Collier's history and point out their logo, mentioning that they may have seen it in the credits of some of those documentaries.

I'd go on to say how well regarded the company was within the education system in the United States – schools, colleges and libraries all carried Collier's products and that they would soon be introduced into the UK as well.

Creating Curiosity and Interest in the Product:
I would explain that what I was about to show them was for their opinions only – that no matter how much they liked what they were about to see, they could not buy it.

Their honesty about the product was the entire point of the evening.

(Always evenings!)

Enticement:
With that made clear, I would pull a compendium volume of the complete Encyclopaedia from my pilot case and explain that early

the following year, this incredible set would become available to schools, colleges and libraries all over the UK.

I would then begin showing what the volumes contained, in detail.

The quality of the hard covers.
The binding.
The paper.
And – always a winner – the six- to ten-part acetate peel-aways of the human body, a frog, and other subjects. I'd hold the entire volume up by a single page to demonstrate the strength of the binding – and so on.

'Qualifying' The Customer:
I explained that later the following year, the set would become available to the public to purchase for their home, but that for our purposes, that evening, the real question was their thoughts on how best to get the message out to the public.

"Which method of advertising works best for you? Advertising in print, on TV, or word of mouth – you know – a friend tells you that you should try something … that sort of thing."

No one will ever admit that advertising works on them – so word of mouth is the answer every time.

"Well, as it happens, Collier's agrees with you! What's the point in spending hundreds of thousands of pounds (dollars) on press and TV ads when most people take no notice?"

Agreement.

"So that's why Collier's is looking for homes in which to place this entire work completely free of charge – for life – on the agreement that after one year, the owner writes a simple one-page letter to the company (show handwritten example) telling us just how useful the set has been. Does that sound like something that might interest you?"

Yes, and enthusiasm a-plenty.

(If not, you pack up and leave with a polite thank-you for their time and input.)

Next, I would take out my clipboard and pen and ask the couple – always the couple – how they believed this free, £500 / $750 (nine months' wages for many!) encyclopaedia set would change their lives.

Five full minutes – often more – would pass while they qualified themselves as worthy owners. Every point carefully noted.

The Sales Pitch in Earnest:
"Now, a factor that has to be accepted is that no encyclopaedia, no matter how carefully constructed, can possibly cover every detail of every subject known to man.

"And so, for this reason, when you or your children are putting together a thesis or other papers, Collier's will support you with their Customer Reference Programme."

Out comes a 24" x 36" presentation sheet.

"A huge team of experts, available to take your questions and offer meaningful advice during up to six calls a year – and this service will be included should you qualify for the programme. You can see the benefit of such a service, I'm sure? How would you use it?"

Of course they would… and so on.
More careful notes on my clipboard.

Any weakness in those responses – thank them for their time, take their name and address for consideration, and leave.

"Okay … there's one other major factor that dogs the entire educational publishing industry, and that is this: No matter how up-to-date an encyclopaedia may be when it goes to press, no sooner is it published than it's out of date!

"Geography, politics, technology, medicine – everything is in a constant state of change. You'd agree with that – right?"

They agree.

"Well, that's why Collier's has introduced The Year Book. This covers all the events of the year and cross-references them back to the original set – for the next ten years. Can you see how that would be useful?"

"Absolutely."

The Clincher:
"So this is where we ask just one small measure of your sincerity to qualify for all the many hundreds of pounds (dollars) worth of facilities I've presented this evening – and that is that you be willing to pay for the Year Books, with no further commitment whatsoever. Does that sound reasonable to you?"

One book a year? No problem.

"Great. So here's one more nice surprise. The Year Books will retail at $25 each, but to programme members, that price will be cut in half – and I'm even going to make that easy for you to handle."

Easy Payments – Made Even Easier (and Fun!):
Out comes Collier's 'Calendar Money Box' – a small metal box with a money slot that advances the day of the month, and another that

advances the month. All the customer needs to do is put a two-shilling piece into the slot each day, and by the end of the month they've saved £4. The agreement asks that this payment be made to the company each month for just three years – not ten – and everything is then paid for. How does that sound?

I never once had a potential customer tell me they couldn't afford to put a two-shilling piece into that calendar box each day.

Paperwork completed. Deal – Done.

And The Take-Away Here?:
The process – applicable in so many situations:
Break the ice
Relax the customer
Sell the company
Make the product interesting – qualify with questions
Enticement (offer / need, etc.)
Be sure they agree with you about the offer and the need
Begin to close the sale with qualifying questions
Close the sale

If at any stage you feel the customer is not with you, it really is best to pack up and move on to the next door.

Many sales people take shortcuts – and then wonder why they fail.

A Meeting of Minds

Ability meets opportunity. Sometimes it pays to think outside the box – in more ways than one.

At an interview with the owner of a small but well-respected cabinet manufacturer, I learned that despite an excellent trade reputation for both quality and service, the business was struggling under the weight of increasing foreign and domestic competition. Retailers spoke highly of the company, but they simply weren't buying in sufficient volume to keep it viable.

I saw real potential in this company, but after talking a while it became clear that he couldn't afford me – and I couldn't afford him.

So I compromised. I offered to work with him for three months as a freelance consultant at a fee that met my needs. I convinced him that this was an investment he could not afford to miss.

The agreement was simple: if, at the end of those three months, he didn't like what he saw, we would part with no hard feelings. I went in, he said, "Go to it," and I did – no holds barred. It didn't take three months for him to realise that I was worth what I had originally asked for – and perhaps a little more.

We had just three months before the trade's major furniture show – manufacturers presenting to retailers large and small from across the UK and beyond.

Following the processes outlined in this book, I met with the sales force, key customers, and people in every corner of the factory and office. Then I set about finding out why this business was underperforming.

Where better to start?

You got it – the customers. All of them.

I sent out a forty-point questionnaire to the company's seven-hundred-plus retailers, asking for their views on key disciplines: the product, the service, the brochures, the price list, their sales representative, customer service staff, the accounts department – and yes, even the drivers.

The owner told me bluntly that we'd be lucky to receive ten responses.

We received well over two hundred.

When I collated the results, the picture became clear. Customers loved the quality of the product but found the designs uninspiring. They praised the service, had mixed views on the sales force, disliked the old-fashioned brochures, and found the price list unnecessarily complicated.

Within two weeks, I knew exactly what needed fixing to get this show back on the road.

Money was tight, so every decision had to be made with cost firmly in mind. I redesigned the cabinets in simple ways that added style, and patented a pull-out tray with a heat-resistant surface, positioned above the sideboard drawers. I modernised the company logo, created contemporary brochures, and redesigned the price list to include thumbnail images of every piece on offer.

All of it was completed in time for that critical furniture show.

Historically, company policy had been to cram as many pieces as possible onto a modest stand. I asked them to be brave – to show less and give each piece room to breathe, and buyers the freedom to move without shuffling sideways.

The result was a resounding success.

Retailers loved the upgrades, and orders poured in. Halfway through the four-day show, the office manager called me and said, "John, we've never had orders like this. Normally it's one of this and three of that - we're getting dozens of orders for full retail displays."

On the strength of that performance, the owner asked me to join the company as Sales Director. I accepted, with one critical proviso: that the bone-deep, brutally honest relationship we had forged would not change simply because he had become my boss.

He agreed.

Over the following year, sales doubled - and then some. The owner then did something he had never done before, not even for himself: he bought me a brand-new Mercedes. Another year on, the company not only had a full order book, but was selling to outlets it had previously never dreamed of approaching.

Ability and opportunity - in perfect harmony.

My biggest takeaway from this experience:
Sometimes everything can look right on the surface. Quality and service may be exemplary – yet performance still disappoints. Often, it's design – in all its forms, from logo to product itself – that quietly holds a company back.

Years later, when Tom Peters published, *The Circle of Innovation,* I smiled in recognition, and in agreement

More on Those
Tough Interview Questions

How to prepare for them:
You will almost certainly be asked some version of the questions below. Not because interviewers enjoy putting candidates on the spot, but because these questions reveal judgement, self-awareness, and maturity under pressure.

The purpose here is not to memorise answers, it's to prepare your thinking so that you respond, honestly, and credibly in the moment.

"Why should we hire you?"
What they're really asking:
What problems do you believe you can solve – and do you understand our problem?

How to prepare:
Frame your answer around outcomes, not attributes.
Avoid generic claims (hard-working, motivated).

Anchor your response in:

- Experience
- Perspective
- Readiness

Think: "What changes for this company if I'm in the role?"

"What did you like least about your last role or manager?"
What they're really asking:
How do you handle frustration and disagreement?
Are you going to get along well with us?

How to prepare:
Speak about situations, not people.
Demonstrate discernment, not resentment.
This is often a trap.
Respond like someone who has already moved on.

"What are your qualifications?"
What they're really asking:
What have you actually learned – formally or otherwise?

How to prepare:
If your education is unconventional, don't apologise for it.
Translate experience into capability. Your confidence here matters more than the list itself.

"What aspects of your job do you consider most important?"
What they're really asking:
Do your priorities align with ours?

How to prepare:
Frame your answer around,

- People
- Performance
- Sustainability

Senior roles are about balance, not heroics.

"Describe a difficult problem you've handled successfully."
What they're really asking:
Can you think clearly under pressure?

How to prepare:
Use a simple structure:

- Situations   (cont'd)

- Actions
- Outcomes
- Learning
- Don't over-dramatise.
- Competence is more persuasive than drama.

"How many hours a week do you work?"
What they're really asking:
Do you understand responsibility – or are you clock-driven?

How to prepare:
Your answer is based around one simple fact: You work as many hours as are necessary. And I do mean *'necessary'*. Don't sell yourself into slavery. I would assert that, 'There's working hard, and there's working 'smart'.

- Avoid bravado.
- Avoid rigidity.
- Signal professionalism
- Commitment whenever needed
- Balance when possible
- Judgement – always

"What kind of salary are you worth?"
What they're really asking:
Do you understand your market value – and yourself?

How to prepare:
Research beforehand.
Know your range.
Be calm.

This is a negotiation, not a test of nerve.

"How long would you stay with the company?"
What they're really asking:
Are you committed – or opportunistic?

How to prepare:
Avoid absolutes.
Express intent, not prediction.
Senior candidates understand that fit determines longevity.

"What is the least relevant job you've held?"
What they're really asking:
Can you extract value from experience?

How to prepare:
Every job teaches something.
Your task is to articulate what.
Perspective beats pedigree here.

"Can we check your references?"
What they're really asking:
Are you transparent – and confident in your past?

How to prepare:
The only correct response is calm acceptance.
If you hesitate, they'll wonder why.

"Why did you leave your last job?"
What they're really asking:
Are you someone who blames – or someone who learns?

How to prepare:
Keep this factual and neutral.

They are seeking out your tolerances and assessing their chances of keeping you.

Focus on:

- Misalignment
- Change
- Growth

Never attack individuals.
Never rehearse old grievances.

A calm explanation signals emotional maturity.

"What is your biggest weakness?"
What they're really asking:
This is the toughest of tough questions to answer – *honestly!*

This is probably *the* toughest interview question to answer without being trite or clichéd. For that reason I am going to afford it all the space it deserves.

How to prepare:
The response should be real and controlled. It should show awareness and responsibility, not self-criticism.

Frame your answer as if this question were:
"Do you know yourself – and how well do you manage your own limitations?"

Avoid:

- Those often used clichés (I work too hard.)
- Flaws that could be perceived as fatal.
- Traits-disguised strengths, (I think I care too much.)

The interviewer is not asking, 'What's wrong with you? They're asking, 'Can you accurately assess yourself, manage risk, and improve under pressure?'

A good answer demonstrates:

- Self-awareness.
- Control.
- Learning in action

A bad answer reveals:

- Insecurity
- Arrogance
- Lack of reflection or rehearsal

The only structure that consistently works:
A strong answer has three parts – in this order:

- A real weakness (not fatal, not cosmetic)
- The cost of that weakness (briefly acknowledged)
- The corrective behaviour (specific and ongoing)

No apologies
No justifications
No virtue signalling

Demonstrate:
Learning, not damage.

Example 1:
Earlier in my career, I underestimated the importance of internal communication.

I focused heavily on results and execution, and I assumed alignment would follow naturally. In reality, it sometimes created unnecessary friction or uncertainty for others.

I've addressed that by building structured communication into how I work – regular check-ins, clearer expectations, and written follow-ups.

It's now something I'm deliberate about, not something I leave to chance.

Example 2:
One of my weaknesses has been impatience when progress stalls.

When I see a clear path forward, I can become frustrated if momentum isn't there – particularly in complex or political environments.

I've learned to manage that by slowing my own response, not forcing the situation. I ask more questions, bring others into the reasoning, and adjust my pace to the organisation rather than the problem. The results are better – and more durable.

Example 3:
My greatest weakness is that I can sometimes take responsibility for problems that aren't mine to solve. Earlier in my career, that led to over-involvement and reduced accountability in others.

I now manage that tendency by being clearer about ownership and outcomes. I support and challenge where needed, but I don't rescue. That shift has improved both performance and trust.

The Take-away:
A good weakness answer reassures the interviewer that you already know where you could fail – you are aware of it and that you have systems in place to prevent it.

Never answer with:

- A trait you're proud of
- A flaw you haven't corrected
- A problem the role can't tolerate
- Things other candidates are likely to say.

If the job requires:
Resilience — don't admit emotional volatility
Attention to detail — don't admit carelessness
People leadership — don't admit poor empathy

Self-awareness is impressive.
Self-harm is not.

Answering questions before you're asked:
A powerful technique to embrace. One of the most effective interview strategies is to address concerns before they're voiced. Particularly if the subject supports you application and you feel the conversation may drift away from the moment.

If you sense uncertainty around your ...
Lack of formal management titles
Varied career history
Industry transition

Then weave your explanation naturally into the conversation. That signals awareness and confidence – not defensiveness.

A Final thought:
Strong interview answers don't sound rehearsed.
They sound considered.

Preparation is not about scripting. It's about knowing what you believe, what you value, and how you think. That's what interviewers are listening for.

The Interview
When all Seems Lost

A personal experience of 'rejection' for age – at 45.
The job was area sales manager (Sales Rep really!) I had travelled 100 miles round trip for the first interview at a local hotel. That interview was held by a recruitment agency that had either been very badly briefed or didn't frame the employer's requirements tightly enough.

I then travelled 300 miles round trip for the second interview at the company plant to be interviewed by the agency and the MD of the company together. The interview went well and I was told there would be a third short list of two.

So, when I got the letter from the agency thanking me for my time, but that 'other candidates were better suited to the client's needs', I called them and asked why I had not been selected. After much hesitation, I was told that the MD thought I was 'too old to fit in with the rest of the sales team'. That was the first time in my life I'd been told I was 'too old' for anything and was not about to accept it.

So I called the MD, told him how much I had enjoyed out meeting, loved the product and wanted to work with him, and how disappointed I was not to have been selected for that final interview. I placed the 'blame' for the 'too old' judgment squarely on the shoulders of agency and made the point that I wasn't selling to the rest of the sales team, I was selling to the customers! He laughed, accepted my point and we met again. He hired me and within a year, he promoted me to sales director.

Failing an Interview for Reasons Unspoken

Personal examples – Ladies first …
My wife was once told that even though she was best qualified for the
job, the interviewer would not hire her because his colleagues would
believe he'd only employed her for her looks! Ouch!

But wait! – I had once done close to the same thing.
Unforgivable surely?

The hidden reason I was unable to voice at the time:
I was working as sales director for a company that supplied its product
to retailers all over the UK. I lived in the middle of England and had a
vacancy for a sales person to cover the whole of Scotland. Sadly, my
previous salesman had died unexpectedly. I needed a presence up
there as soon as possible and so conducted initial interviews tucked
away in one corner of the company's annual trade exhibition stand.

Unannounced, a beautiful young lady approached me saying she'd just
heard about the vacancy and would appreciate the opportunity to
discussing the post. Turned out she was by far the best candidate.

As she left the stand my sales guys were keen to give me the nudge
with the typical, 'No doubt who's getting the job, then!' type quips.

So why didn't she get the job?:
The fact was, my wife of some forty years was suffering a serious depres-
sion. She was in her mid-fifties and often confided in me that she was
hating 'looking like an old bag.' She wasn't of course, she was actually
aging incredibly well, but she just didn't see it that way.

Imagine then, how insecure and more deeply depressed and even
perhaps suspicious she would have been every time it was necessary for
me to spend a couple of nights away in Scotland, knowing I had a bubbly
and beautiful young woman by my side all day and with whom I would

sometimes be sharing the same hotel. I just couldn't do it to her – and so another candidate won the day.

This is not a defence of such decisions – only an acknowledgement that leadership sometimes carries conflicts no arbitrary process can fully resolve. It remains one of the hardest decisions of my career – and one that reminds me how carefully power must be exercised.

The High Price Paid
For Getting Things Wrong

A UK Giant Falls from Grace

Being careful what you wish for:
During our mid-twenties, my wife spotted an advertisement in the evening paper for an Area Sales Manager and suggested I apply. I laughed out loud when I saw the brand.

In 1970s UK, this king of all bed manufacturers held brand recognition rivalling Hoover. They commanded around a quarter of the national market, and proudly boasted the Royal Warrant: By Appointment to Her Majesty The Queen – and The Queen Mother.

What chance did I stand? On application, my CV disclosed a career that included selling meat pies to pubs, clubs and chip shops; encyclopaedias door-to-door, and cleaning chemicals to local industry – the latter two on a commission-only.

I had no connections in the retail furniture trade and no knowledge of the bedding business whatsoever. What chance would I stand against established industry figures with contacts galore and product knowledge up the yin-yang?

But… just to prove my ever-loving wife wrong (this once), I applied. She, of course, smiled from ear to ear when the interview notification arrived.

Now I'm thinking: I must be the wild card – the outsider extraordinaire. What on earth were they thinking?

That said – boy, did I prepare! I created a presentation folder of sales achievements and letters of praise from the industrial chemicals company plus heaven knows what else I found to include – but whatever it was, it worked. I got the job.

Why?!

I was about to find out.

My initiation had been carefully orchestrated, and my first ever brand-new company car duly delivered. I was quite sure I had died and gone to heaven.

Little me – Area Sales Manager for this incredibly prestigious brand.

Suited and booted, clean and pristine, sales presenter at the ready and product training memorised, I made my first call: a small, mom-and-dad furniture store.

I introduced myself proudly – and received a cringe and a fingered hex from the owner in response.

With it came a question I was ill-prepared for:

"Oh yes – and where were you before this, then? Heinz Beans? Campbell's Soup? A second-hand car salesman perhaps? Not the furniture trade, I'll wager!"

I was completely on my back foot and couldn't understand the animosity towards a representative of a company that sold a quarter of all beds in the UK.

Thankfully, the man could see my shock. He relaxed, smiled, and invited me into his office for a nice cup of tea – Britain's cure for all ills.

Early learning:
Sitting comfortably at his desk, he explained that the company had recently been acquired by a large steel corporation. They had installed an all-new senior management team and had changed the long-respected specification of their beds – retaining only their famous, patented springing unit.

Worse still, it was widely known throughout the trade that the company was now replacing its entire sales force with grocery-trade rookies of the 'stack-'em-high and sell-'em-fast' variety.

I knew from my training and factory tours that the company had recently made dramatic changes to mattress construction – moving from traditional fillings to an all-foam construction. These new mattresses could withstand over a million passes on a pressure roller – but the trade were having none of it.

My buyer continued:

"The Brand was the best in the trade until this. Substantial, heavy beds – the top end needed two people to lift them. Now they blow away in the breeze! I hear one store owner saw a little old lady running off down the street with one!"

Beyond the humour, it was painful to hear – especially when he told me I had taken the job from a fifty-nine-year-old he considered a friend, who had been with the firm for over thirty years.

Corporate arrogance & the downward spiral:
So here was a brand that, in a crowded marketplace, commanded a massive share of the UK market. How, then, could it fall to just 6% over the next four years?

Here's how:
Behind closed doors – and with no meaningful retail research – the owner/CEO decided that a high-quality foam wrap around the

spring unit would offer a longer-lasting mattress. It would weigh a quarter as much, be cleaner and cheaper to manufacture, and easier to handle.

Retailers would love it – lighter weight, non-allergenic, over a million roller passes, and still carrying that all-important brand.

Manufacturing was transformed: greater speed, lower costs, less space per unit, fewer skilled operatives, and simpler distribution.

To accommodate the anticipated surge in volume, the company opened a massive new factory – a move that took them out of the market for three months. This in a trade where every competitor delivered within two weeks.

Imagine how swiftly the company's competitors moved to fill those empty shop-floor spaces.

For other major-brand bed manufacturers, it was a dream come true.

Was the company board worried? Not particularly. They believed their brand dominance would force retailers back – because consumers would demand it.

WRONG.

When the new feather-weight product finally arrived – virtually unannounced – retailers saw half the product (by weight) for the same money.

It was a disaster.

The CEO's solution – *New management:* The newly appointed 'toothpaste and canned-soup' crowd concluded that the old sales force simply didn't know how to sell. They were brand-dependent order-takers.

"Sack the lot and bring in new blood."

Enter — me.

A man who had sold expensive encyclopaedias door-to-door. A man who sold cleaning chemicals to hard-nosed mechanics at four times their previous spend. A man who could sell himself.

That's why I got the job.

The vultures circle:
Historically, the company had sold exclusively to independent retailers and, by exception, the Co-op.

Now they were desperate.

Their retail base had deserted them. Large chains and out-of-town big-box stores clamoured for the brand – and its excess capacity – at a price.

Back to my first day.

The company had launched a promotion: a double bed drawer divan at £89.95 trade, with TV advertising at £149.95 retail.

Sounds good – right?

NOPE.

Two weeks later, a TV advert appeared from a major retail chain:

A man kneels to inspect the drawers, looks up and says:
"Agree our price and we'll buy five thousand sets."

Voice-over:
"Drawer divans– £99.95 – at Williams. Where else!"

They were *retailing* the same bed for £10 more than independents were paying *wholesale*.

This, in a trade built on 100% mark-ups.

Need I say more?

The company chased volume everywhere. The sales force was slashed. Five Area Sales Directors became two. Teams were gutted.

And me?

I was fortunate. Much of my patch was North Wales – no big-box stores at all. A temporary cushion.

Did I hide behind it? – No.

I became a nuisance. I pleaded. I relayed what customers were shouting. Eventually, I left – still delivering solid numbers. Not long after, a third board sold the company. The business was never again the powerhouse it once was. As I write they don't even make the top ten. A casualty of corporate arrogance – a disease still rampant in businesses of all types today.

Years later, I met one of the Area Sales Directors. He asked if I knew my head-office nickname. I didn't. He laughed: "Moulton – The Irritant. You were always a thorn in their side."

I think he meant it kindly. I was pleased I'd made some impression.

The moral of this story:
Corporate arrogance is a killer.
Volume is vanity. Profit is sanity.
Listen to your people.
Listen to your customers.
No company is indispensable.

Greed or Flailing Desperation?

Let me give you a personal example of how the volume-discount-quality battle played out with one of the companies I worked with.

I was sales and marketing manager with an upholstery manufacturer that produced nice quality show-wood frame cottage-style suites for old folks. They were well respected in the trade, but the new senior management had taken them down the volume-at-a-price route, trying to get out of a huge debt crisis caused partly by recession and partly by prior mis-management.

I joined them just as volume was increasing into group retail outlets that they had never served before, the business secured at heavily discounted prices by the new MD who had 'the right contacts'. His business model drove production up to all-time highs, in fact the company was soon quoting twelve and sixteen weeks delivery rather than the customary six.

Income went through the roof, but profitability remain stagnant due to the discounts being offer to secure that volume. So pressure from the bank to reduce their overdraft just got heavier as the months went by.

Add to this that small independent retailers were suffering even longer delivery times because the big boys were not only enjoying far better deals but jumping the delivery line and claiming the bulk of the production, too.

My job was to manage the sales force servicing those independent retailers – often the smaller mom and dad outlets of which there were around seven thousand in the UK at the time.

At a meeting with the board, I suggested trying something different: a product with a little meat on the bone that would be available only to independents, and therefore not subject to the crippling discounts demanded by the groups.

I got the go-ahead and began working with an external design team to create something genuinely special.

When the MD saw the prototype, he agreed it was lovely – but assured me it would never sell, because the direct cost meant a trade price some 40% higher than anything they had ever offered before.

Nonetheless, I was allowed to proceed.

Product completed, I moved to photography. This was usually done in a simple studio room-set, with little more than a picture or a plant for decoration. But I needed more – and so asked for permission to use a room in the chairman's rather palatial manor-style home.

Permission was granted. The result? Very classy!

Dragging a company into the light:
Quite apart from the more shapely design, and a broader offer in terms of pieces available, it was also the first product ever to be given an actual name. A typical product name was 'Model 310'. The new models were 'The Sandringham' in natural beech and 'The Balmoral' in mahogany – with brass castor front feet.

It was an instant hit with independents, who also recognised that its market demographic began much earlier – around age 45–50 rather than 70.

Buoyed by the products early success, the MD proudly placed the suite centre-stage at the national furniture trade exhibition. He was confident the group buyers would walk straight past it once they learned the price – but promised that if any showed interest, they would be told that the complexity of the design limited discounts to around 5–10%. The promise lasted less than a day.

The groups loved it. They promised vast volumes for the right price – and by the end of the day, 15–25% discounts were being casually bandied about.

I wish I could say it ended well – but instead, this story illustrates how volume can become a disease.

The MD was convinced that over time he could make the company's products indispensable and force prices upward.

Well … they say the graveyard is full of indispensable people, and I say the same is true of products and businesses, too.

The company went down with a full order book, the day the bank pulled the plug.

AND NOW

A little something
that has irritated me for years!

CAUTION!

Life on the road will never be the same
once you have read this final offering!

WHEN OPPORTUNITY KNOCKS
BUT THERE'S NOBODY HOME!

Opportunities Missed

First, let me hammer a few stakes in the ground:
One of the most important components of advertising is placement!
You want the top right corner of your local paper,
You want a right-hand page of a magazine,
You want to be the first or the last commercial during TV program
breaks… and on …

Placement:
Placement is perhaps even more important than content. Even
horrible advertising causes a reaction – it becomes memorable for its
diabolicability (I just made that word up!) But no matter how good
or how bad any advert may be, it's pointless if nobody sees it …

Obvious, right?

So why do so many companies throw away one of the most highly
efficient, highly productive and cost-effective advertising platforms
available to them?

Opportunity Knocks:
Let's take a look at one remarkable advertising opportunity that you
pay for once – probably way less that $2,000 – and has the potential
to be seen by thousands of people, often for ten or more years ahead.

A blank canvas, ten feet high by seven feet wide that is under the
noses of thousands of people who often cannot escape gazing at it for
quite some time – in fact, there are times when turning their head
away from it could quite literally kill them!

SO WHERE IS THIS PLATFORM TO DIE FOR?

>   >   >

One For The Road

If you haven't guessed already, I'm talking about the back of a wagon, truck, van, trailer – whatever. And even when companies do think to splash a little paint on the tailgate, they often miss the mark by a country mile.

There is a great deal of time wasted on our roads.

Traffic jams are unavoidable. And in those idle moments when we are forced to slow down, all we have to look at is the back of the vehicle in front of us. But we're not just waiting – we are noticing.

The back of a commercial vehicle is one of the most valuable advertising spaces a company will ever own. It sits at eye level. It has a captive audience. It travels through towns, cities, industrial estates, motorways, villages, and suburbs. It is seen by customers, suppliers, employees, and future recruits.

And yet, astonishingly often, it says little or nothing at all.

Sometimes it's just a name. Sometimes a logo. Sometimes a phone number too small to read. And quite often, it's blank.

Which is odd, when you think about it, because if what we see sparks curiosity, we remember it.

That is how selling really works.

Years ago, I was stuck behind one such vehicle for miles. It was clean, well maintained, and unmistakably professional. Yet the company name on the back told me nothing. No story. No invitation. No clue.

On the side panel – nothing more. On the cab door, finally, a hint: *General Haulage*. About as evocative as, "Joe's Potatoes."

Curiosity had the better of me, so I did what most people wouldn't bother to do. I looked them up.

What I discovered was remarkable.

This was not a company that merely transported goods. This was a business capable of moving extraordinary industrial structures – loads that demand bespoke trailers, route surveys, permits, bridge calculations, escort vehicles, and planning measured in months rather than hours.

And yet, from the driver's seat behind one of their vehicles, you would never know any of it.

The back of that wagon told no story. It made no claim. It sparked no curiosity. And so the truth of what they did – the scale, complexity, and competence – passed unnoticed by thousands of people every day – some of whom may actually be desperate for their service, but just don't know where to look.

There is a world of difference between being capable – and being seen to be capable.

I ached for this company to share some of the amazing photographs I saw on their website. So easy to share, out there, on the back of that wagon, for all to see just how amazing they are.

Some companies understand this instinctively. They use that same slab of metal to make us smile, to make us think, or simply to make us look again. With a message that says, 'This is who we are. This is what we do. And this is how to find us.'

Others leave the space empty, Some for good reason, I'm sure, but others simply haven't given the matter a moments though.

Corporate ego often dictates you'll see a company name or logo nothing more and heaven forbid they should tell you what they do or how to reach them.

The point here is about awareness.

In my experience, leaders are too often like that vehicle ahead of you in traffic. They sit directly in front of us, every day – missing opportunities. The chance to make an impression or leave none at all. A manifestation of opportunity wasted.

Some notice what's missing. The clarity. The intent. The culture. The unspoken expectations. The spaces where something meaningful could be said – or done – and isn't.

The difference is rarely intelligence.

It is attention.

The ability to actually see. To notice what is absent as much as what is present. To understand that what goes unsaid can damage a company's opportunities for growth.

Throughout this book we've talked about readiness. About fit. About timing. About understanding how organisations should and could work for the better.

This final example is a reminder that small things often carry enormous weight. That a blank canvas – whether on the back of a wagon or at the heart of a management role – is not neutral. It's either used, or it's wasted.

It is worth remembering that what you choose not to say – or do – is often the loudest message of all.

And So, Full Circle …

Earlier, I asked you to pause, write down, and set aside your response to this tough interview question:

"What would your first ninety days look like?"

Now is the time to return to your answer.

If your journey through these pages has given you clarity, confidence, or a new perspective, it should be reflected here – in what you choose next – how you frame it, and why it matters to you and those around you.

That answer is no longer hypothetical. It's a signal of your readiness for what comes next.

Make it count

Reflections

The single most important thing
I ever learned in business

During my working life, I had the privilege of working for many different companies – more than I once expected. In hindsight, that experience became an education no textbook offered. I witnessed management at its best and at its most painfully flawed. From the trenches, I learned not only how things should be done, but how disastrously wrong things can go when leadership loses its way.

For that, I am genuinely grateful.

Every organisation taught me something. Every role, every culture, every misstep added another layer of understanding. I met people at all levels who cared deeply, and others – from shop floor to board-room – who were simply 'getting on with it'.

Both mattered. Both shaped my view.

That lived experience is the reason this book was written – *for you*.

Because the single most important thing I learned is this:

Given the opportunity, the role of sales director carries an extraordinary level of influence – and with it, a rare responsibility.

No other position in a company offers the same freedom to roam, to connect, and to listen. Not only to customers and the sales team, but to every individual who helps keep the machine running. Even chief executives rarely experience that breadth of access – and sadly, many wouldn't thank you for it. At the very top, 'truth' can become a rarity, or even disappears all but completely.

But for the sales director it's different.

A familiar face on the factory floor. A trusted presence in production, finance, administration, and leadership meetings alike. Officially there to check on key orders or customer service and of course the numbers – but in reality, working hard to understand people. To build trust. To untangle problems before they get out of control. To influence hearts and minds at all levels of the business.

Such is the opportunity that awaits you.

When your ability meets its moment, and 'the fit' feels as natural as a pair of well-worn shoes, you will find yourself in a position not just to lead sales – but to help shape the very character of the business itself. And that, in my personal experience, is as rewarding as working life gets.

If you choose to lead with curiosity, courage, and care, you'll find that the title matters far less to you than the trust you earn – and the change that follows.

Wishing you every success

About The Author

John D. Moulton spent more than five decades rising from door-to-door salesman to senior sales leadership roles within major UK manufacturing organisations. Known for his people-first leadership style, he built and led sales teams, developed and coached leaders, and navigated the realities of growth, restructuring, and cultural change from the inside.

Now retired from corporate life, he draws on lived experience to write candidly about leadership, accountability, and the decisions that shape careers. *The Instant Sales Director* is informed by lessons learned in boardrooms, interviews, and in the field – where strategy meets reality.

NOTES